THE POWER OF AGREEMENT

DR. ETHAN W. OGLETREE SR.

Community Services Press
Washington, DC

COMMUNITY SERVICES PRESS

Community Services Press
2101 N St., NW, Suite T-1
Washington, DC 20037

310-406-8300
www.communityservicespress.com

For seminar and lecture information please contact:
New Destiny Praise and Worship Center
4170 West Greens Road
Houston, Texas 77066

281-580-8686 / Fax 281-580-8601

Printed in the United States of America
18 17 16 15 14   1 2 3 4 5

ISBN 13: 978-0-9841286-9-3

Editing by J. McCrary, CSP Editorial Services, j@jmccrary.com
Cover design by Christopher Lewis, www.icreatespot.com
Interior by Westcom Associates, westcomassociates@mac.com

Contents

Acknowledgments

I give thanks and praise to God, whom I humbly serve in agreement with His will and design for my life. With Him, all things are possible.

I would like to thank Pamela, my wife, for being my supporter and for joining me on the journey that God has for us. The power of agreement in our home and our ministry will ultimately bring glory to God. I will love you always.

I would like to thank Ethan Jr., J'Von, and Jasmine—my children for teaching me to love like our Father in heaven.

My gratitude to all the great men and women of faith that have mentored me, given me advice and support during my ministry. Your wisdom has been invaluable in this journey.

Special thanks to Michael Vezo and J. McCrary for their invaluable assistance in making the dream of publishing my first book a reality. You were a welcome resource at the right time.

My love and gratitude to the New Destiny Praise and Worship Center family for their trust in and devotion to me as their Pastor.

"I keep asking that the God of our Lord Jesus Christ, the glorious Father, may give you the Spirit of wisdom and revelation, so that you may know him better. I pray that the eyes of your heart may be enlightened in order that you may know the hope to which he has called you, the riches of his glorious inheritance in his holy people, and his incomparably great power for us who believe."

Ephesians 1:17-19 (New International Version)

Introduction

"For I know the plans I have for you,"
declares the Lord, "plans to prosper you
and not to harm you, plans to give you a
hope and a future."

Jeremiah 29:11 (New International Version)

*Y*ou are reading *The Power of Agreement* because you are on the path to become a leader in your community, in your church, and in your family. Perhaps you are a new graduate, planning a life that matters. You have the faith and intelligence to make a positive difference in this world, and you are ready for a mentor and some guidance to fulfill your destiny.

Perhaps you are already far along this path. You may be a church leader, an elder or teacher, perhaps. You may be a business owner or a community volunteer. Most certainly, others already look up to you.

You all share one certainty: This is not a journey that you can attempt alone. None of you can walk along this path by yourselves. Becoming a leader involves building layers of relationships and agreements—with those who mentor you, with employers, with partners who work alongside you, and with those you guide.

Your most important relationship is the one you build with God.

You must be in agreement with God to truly become the leader that you can become. Remember that the path you're following is supposed to lead to heaven; isn't that your ultimate goal?

With agreement, we become one—with God, with our brothers and sisters, with our better selves, and with our spouses. We become empowered to live productive, fruitful lives for the kingdom.

In the following chapters, we will study the spiritual power of agreement and the scriptures that explain God's purpose and expectations. We will also study agreements and practices from some of the biggest corporations in the world, and understand how the same principles underlie their successes and failures.

Chapter One

The Power of Agreement

It's Symbiotic

None of us lives in a vacuum. Every aspect of our lives is affected by agreements we make with corporations, family, friends, fellow church members, and most certainly God. We are never totally on our own or in sole control of our lives.

When you buy something from a retailer and use your debit or credit card, you and the store have an unspoken agreement. Your plastic card will have enough cash or credit backing it to pay for an item. The store is selling it as represented (price, condition, warranty, availability). You both agree that the retailer will do no harm to you. The store is not going to charge you twice or sell a copy of your credit card information to the highest bidder. The clerk is not going to pack your bag with rocks when you're looking the other way, and he won't slide your new shoes under the counter to sell again.

We take this unspoken agreement for granted.

So how do we feel about what happened at Target, one of our nation's largest retailers? From the day before Thanksgiving until the week before Christmas in 2013, Target ignored warnings of a potential data breach that affected possibly 110 million customers— maybe including you or someone in your family. When you slid your plastic card through the slot at the Target checkout, hackers—thieves!—were able to read the magnetic strip on your card, steal the information and sell it to other thieves.

Prior to this happening, as part of their security measures to protect consumer data, Target made a written agreement with an anti-hacking security firm that specialized in monitoring suspicious data activity. When this watchdog firm told Target that they'd been hacked and they needed to turn a switch on their computer system to block the hackers, the bigwigs at Target's headquarters disregarded the agreement and ignored their experts. The thieves stole information from every swipe we made for weeks.

The data theft could have been stopped in three days if Target had paid attention when their security department was first warned of the breach.

Our agreement with a trusted retailer was broken, and some of us were harmed financially. We are fortunate that most of us were just scared and no harm was done to our wallets.

Good changes may actually come from the aftermath. The retailers are making agreements with each other to find better ways of protecting us. Newer, more secure ways of paying are being perfected, and we'll be safer in the future.

In this chapter, we're going to study the unspoken and spoken agreements that God makes with us. We will learn how he protects us from the biblical equivalent of hackers, even when it's not obvious that he's doing so. It's important that we learn to listen to the voice of God.

> *"Two are better than one; because they have a good reward for their labour. For if they fall, the one will lift up his fellow: but woe to him that is alone when he falleth; for he hath not another to help him up. Again, if two lie together, then they have heat: but how can one be warm alone? And if one prevail against him, two shall withstand him; and a threefold cord is not quickly broken."*

> Ecclesiastes 4:9-12 (King James Version)

"Can two walk together, except
they be agreed?"

Amos 3:3 (King James Version)

From the beginning of time, God desired agreement with man.

God created us in His image, complete with intellect and emotions, so that we can connect and come into agreement with Him about worldly things. When God created man, He wanted someone to walk with Him and agree with Him, building a symbiotic relationship of mutual benefit and dependence.

The scripture teaches that two are better than one, but the two cannot walk together unless they agree.

One of my favorite parables is about a man who lived with his family in a house next to a large forest. One day, the man took his son's hand and led him through the backyard and deep into the woods until they reached the darkest center of the forest.

"Do you know your way home from here?" the father asked.

"No," the son replied,

"Do you know where you are?"

"No."

"Are you afraid?"

"No."

"Are you lost?"

"No," the son said calmly.

The father scratched his head, confused. Although the boy was aware that he did not know where he was or how to get back home, he certainly was not scared.

The father asked, "Well, son, why aren't you afraid?

"Because I am with you," the son smiled.

The son was not rattled by his uncertain circumstances because he absolutely believed that his father knew what he was doing. All the son had to do was trust and agree with his father, and everything would work out fine.

Our Father never wanted us to be lost in this large world. Though Adam and Eve were in the Garden of Eden, God wanted them to have dominion over the Earth. God had no fears or worries because He knew they were with Him. God created man so we could walk with Him in agreement.

We Christians need to trust God and agree with Him about our own situations more often. Once we are in agreement with Him, our stress levels will drop, and we will be ready to calmly receive God's

We must learn to live together as brothers or perish together as fools.

—Martin Luther King, Jr.

blessings. We will know that everything will be all right as long as we have our Father in Heaven.

Not only did God desire the covenant of agreement, he also designed it. Why do you think God allowed Adam to name all the things He created? It was because God knew that whatever Adam decided, it would be pleasing to Him.

> *Now the LORD God had formed out of the ground all the beasts of the field and all the birds of the air. He brought them to the man to see what he would name them; and whatever the man called each living creature, that was its name. So the man gave names to all the livestock, the birds of the air and all the beasts of the field.*
>
> *But for Adam no suitable helper was found. So the LORD God caused the man to fall into a deep sleep; and while he was sleeping, he took one of the man's ribs and closed up the place with flesh. Then the LORD God made a woman from the rib he had taken out of the man, and he brought her to the man.*

Genesis 2:19-22 (New International Version)

Early in creation, God said, "It is not good for man to be alone," and He established agreement when He formed Eve, someone to agree with Adam.

He also designed agreement because he wanted a priestly measure. God called Moses to lead His people, the Israelites, but Moses said:

"I am slow of speech and tongue."

"O LORD, please send someone else to do it."

Then the LORD's anger burned against Moses and he said, "What about your brother, Aaron the Levite? I know he can speak well. He is already on his way to meet you, and his heart will be glad when he sees you. You shall speak to him and put words in his mouth; I will help both of you speak and will teach you what to do. He will speak to the people for you, and it will be as if he were your mouth and as if you were God to him."

Exodus 4:10, 13-16 (New International Version)

When God has a divine purpose for your life, agree with Him and He will provide the resources needed to fulfill His divine purpose for your life.

God's agreement with Moses was fulfilled when Aaron, glad to see his brother, was willing to work with him and speak on his behalf.

God also wanted agreement because He knew that man would suffer pain and tears in this worldly life. That is why He gave us the examples of Ruth and Naomi:

> *Then Naomi said to her two daughters-in-law, "Go back, each of you, to your mother's home. May the LORD show kindness to you, as you have shown to your dead and to me. May the LORD grant that each of you will find rest in the home of another husband."*
>
> *Then she kissed them and they wept aloud and said to her, "We will go back with you to your people."*
>
> *But Naomi said, "Return home, my daughters. Why would you come with me? Am I going to have any more sons, who could become your husbands? Return home, my daughters; I am too old to have another husband. Even if I thought there was still hope for me—*

even if I had a husband tonight and then gave birth to sons would you wait until they grew up? Would you remain unmarried for them? No, my daughters. It is more bitter for me than for you, because the LORD's hand has gone out against me!"

At this they wept again. Then Orpah kissed her mother-in-law good-by, but Ruth clung to her.

"Look," said Naomi, "your sister-in-law is going back to her people and her gods. Go back with her."

But Ruth replied, "Don't urge me to leave you or to turn back from you. Where you go I will go, and where you stay I will stay. Your people will be my people and your God my God. Where you die I will die, and there I will be buried. May the LORD deal with me, be it ever so severely, if anything but death separates you and me." When Naomi realized that Ruth was determined to go with her, she stopped urging her.

Ruth 1:8-18 (New International Version)

Unfortunately, when pain and trouble come, mistakes are made or money is low, often those who are supposed to be in agreement with us flee because they aren't willing to handle the distress. They don't have Ruth's strength and enduring love.

The story, of Elisha walking in agreement with Elijah is a long story but one that's worthy of your time.

When the Lord was about to take Elijah up to heaven in a whirlwind, Elijah and Elisha were on their way from Gilgal. Elijah said to Elisha, "Stay here; the Lord has sent me to Bethel."

But Elisha said, "As surely as the Lord lives and as you live, I will not leave you." So they went down to Bethel.

The company of the prophets at Bethel came out to Elisha and asked, "Do you know that the Lord is going to take your master from you today?"

"Yes, I know," Elisha replied, "so be quiet."

Then Elijah said to him, "Stay here, Elisha; the Lord has sent me to Jericho."

And he replied, "As surely as the Lord lives and as you live, I will not leave you." So they went to Jericho.

The company of the prophets at Jericho went up to Elisha and asked him, "Do you know that the Lord is going to take your master from you today?"

"Yes, I know," he replied, "so be quiet."

Then Elijah said to him, "Stay here; the Lord has sent me to the Jordan."

And he replied, "As surely as the Lord lives and as you live, I will not leave you." So the two of them walked on.

Fifty men from the company of the prophets went and stood at a distance, facing the place where Elijah and Elisha had stopped at the Jordan. Elijah took his cloak, rolled it up and struck the water with it. The water divided to the right and to the left, and the two of them crossed over on dry ground.

When they had crossed, Elijah said to

Elisha, *"Tell me, what can I do for you before I am taken from you?"*

"Let me inherit a double portion of your spirit," Elisha replied.

"You have asked a difficult thing," Elijah said, *"yet if you see me when I am taken from you, it will be yours—otherwise, it will not."*

You never fail until you stop trying.
—Albert Einstein

As they were walking along and talking together, suddenly a chariot of fire and horses of fire appeared and separated the two of them, and Elijah went up to heaven in a whirlwind. Elisha saw this and cried out, "My father! My father! The chariots and horsemen of Israel!" And Elisha saw him no more. Then he took hold of his garment and tore it in two.

Elisha then picked up Elijah's cloak that had fallen from him and went back and stood on the bank of the Jordan. He took the cloak that had fallen from Elijah and struck the water with it. "Where now is the Lord, the God of Elijah?" he asked. When he struck the water, it divided to the right and to the left, and he crossed over.

The company of the prophets from Jericho, who were watching, said, "The spirit of Elijah is resting on Elisha." And they went to meet him and bowed to the ground before him.

2 Kings 2:1-15 (New International Version)

Because Elijah left his cloak and some of his spirit for Elisha, we conclude that God wanted man to be able to make an agreement that could endure after his death.

It is interesting how the Israelites redefined agreement. God gave them instructions that they should not mingle with certain types of people who might corrupt them, they should never forget where they came from, or worship any idols. God wanted them to remember that the world has not always been good to them. He gave them covenants and commandments to live by, and reminded them of their beginnings and their deliverance.

"Then the LORD said to Moses, "Write down these words, for in accordance with these words I have made a covenant with you and with Israel."

Exodus 34:27(New International Version)

They literally knew the fear of God; they knew they needed to agree with His commandments or the consequences would be dire.

While Moses was on Mount Sinai, however, the Israelites quickly forgot who God was and broke their agreement with him. They went against His specific instructions and created a golden idol to worship. Agreeing that the Israelites were a "stiff-necked people," Moses talked a wrathful God out of destroying them all on the spot.

If truth be told, we are stiff-necked in the same way. We have forgotten our agreement with God. We have forgotten that He is our deliverer. We say terrible things to God: "If you deliver me this one last time, I'll be at church all the time...."

When people are divided, the only solution is agreement.
–John Hume

So if God desired and designed agreement, why did he allow man to redefine it? To answer this, let's explore His interactions with our dreams.

Men do not share the same dream.

God warns you to be careful with whom you share your dreams. People will steal or attempt to squelch your dream, and He will stop speaking to you if you share it too soon or with the wrong person. People may not like how you dream; they may feel threatened or jealous. It is easy for them to agree with you when you are not dreaming, but when you start sharing your dreams, they may turn against you.

Living according to your dreams can bring extraordinary pain. I would like to caution you that what God reveals tends to reflect the opposite of our present circumstances. Nevertheless, dreams also come with uncommon favor and protection by God.

> *Joseph had a dream, and when he told it to his brothers, they hated him all the more. He said to them, "Listen to this dream I had: We were binding sheaves of grain out in the field when suddenly my sheaf rose and stood upright, while your sheaves gathered around mine and bowed down to it."*
>
> *His brothers said to him, "Do you intend to reign over us? Will you actually rule us?"*

And they hated him all the more because of his dream and what he had said.

Then he had another dream, and he told it to his brothers. "Listen," he said, "I had another dream, and this time the sun and moon and eleven stars were bowing down to me."

Genesis 37:5(New International Version)

When Joseph revealed his dream to his brothers, his life took a turn for the worse. His brothers jealously plotted to murder him, but with the Lord's protection, he was only sold into slavery.

(Genesis 37:26-28; 39:1).

In the midst of extraordinary pain comes extraordinary protection, but you must develop extraordinary patience.

Joseph's life veered through wild ups and downs from then on. He was favored by his first master, but then he was falsely accused by his master's wife and sent to prison. By interpreting other prisoners' dreams correctly, Joseph was promised release by one of them, the Pharaoh's wine cup bearer, who then forgot and left him in prison for two more years.

When the Pharaoh had a dream, the cup bearer remembered Joseph, and he was called to interpret the dream. By recognizing the dream as God's plans for Egypt, Joseph was able to correctly interpret it, and he impressed the Pharaoh with his wisdom. As a result, the Pharaoh put Joseph in charge of all Egypt—making him a CEO to the Pharaoh's Chairman of the Board—and fulfilling both of their dreams.

Though Joseph was betrayed by those closest to him and he suffered much pain and loneliness, he never lost hope in his dream.

Trust in dreams, for in them is hidden the gate to eternity.
–Kahlil Gibran

Living according to your dreams will produce extraordinary abilities. I want you to read this carefully: Your obedience, coupled with the power of God, creates a harmony in the spirit realm that brings the threat of doom and terror onto your enemies--to the point of their defeat. Because God is committed to seeing that His will be done, there should be no fear of failure. Walking in divine destiny alongside God unlocks your greatest ideas and creativity and gives you the energy to manifest them.

The power of a dream (and the danger of revealing

it) allowed Gideon to defeat the Midianites. God told Gideon to eavesdrop on an enemy camp:

> *Gideon arrived just as a man was telling a friend his dream. "I had a dream," he was saying. "A round loaf of barley bread came tumbling into the Midianite camp. It struck the tent with such force that the tent overturned and collapsed."*

> *His friend responded, "This can be nothing other than the sword of Gideon son of Joash, the Israelite. God has given the Midianites and the whole camp into his hands."*

> *When Gideon heard the dream and its interpretation, he bowed down and worshiped. He returned to the camp of Israel and called out, "Get up! The Lord has given the Midianite camp into your hands."*

> Judges 7:13-15 (New International Version)

Living according to your dreams requires an extraordinary relationship. The kingdom of God is expanding, and He is calling more people forward to fulfill His purposes. You must be willing to embrace the dream that He gives you and go forth in all confidence that He is with you.

> *Roll your works upon the Lord [commit and trust them wholly to Him; He will cause your thoughts to become agreeable to His will, and] so shall your plans be established* and *succeed.*
>
> Proverbs 16:3 (Amplified Bible)

In addition, your dreams must be born within you, not borrowed from others. God has given each person a unique dream so they will have a purpose in life as well as to benefit His kingdom.

> *For I know the plans I have for you,"* *declares the LORD, "plans to prosper you and not to harm you, plans to give you hope and a future.*
>
> Jeremiah 29:11 (New International Version)

When you accept the dream He gives you, it is an agreement, a covenant you make with the Lord. You must set aside time every day to consult with God for new insight and revelations on how to get closer to your dream. When you work on your dream, you show God that you are willing to sacrifice all you have for His purpose.

Your work also proves to him that He can trust you with a large blessing, and it will always be available for His use. Without proper sacrifice, you will lack the spiritual favor and authority that comes with walking with Him in your own divine destiny. The stories we've already studied show Gideon put his life on the line, Joseph lost his freedom, and God gave us Jesus to see His dream of salvation come true for us.

When we can't dream any longer, we die.

–Emma Goldman

What are you willing to sacrifice for the sake of your dreams? All God requires is for us to regularly give our time, tithes, and offerings (or more simply put, obedience) to automatically trigger His release of the extraordinary into your life.

> *God says, "Bring the whole tithe into the storehouse, that there may be food in my house. Test me in this," says the LORD Almighty, "and see if I will not throw open the floodgates of heaven and pour out so much blessing that you will not have room enough for it.*
>
> Malachi 3:10 (New International Version)

If you diligently obey this command, you will continuously be a blessed person!

Here is what God has for you if you build your dreams upon faithful tithing and offering:

> *"And I will rebuke the devourer for your sakes, So that he will not destroy the fruit of your ground, Nor shall the vine fail to bear fruit for you in the field,"*

> *Says the LORD OF HOSTS; "And all nations will call you blessed, for you will be a delightful land," Says the LORD OF HOSTS.*

Malachi 3:11-12 (New King James Version)

God wants you to know, however, that if you do spoil your dream, he will give you another. Don't give up!

God will always be your support, and whatever you lay your hands upon shall prosper.

Joseph's gift of dreaming and interpreting dreams connected him with his exalted life as the leader of Egypt—but only after slavery and prison. We learn from the middlemen in Joseph's story that a dreamer will draw two types of people to him, haters (his brothers, his master's wife, and the baker) and celebrators (the cupbearer and the Pharaoh). As a dreamer, you need to add more celebrators to your crowd. A bad habit that we all fall into, unfortunately, is being competitive rather than supportive. We cynically wait to see who's going the distance rather than support their dream. God teaches us that we should not automatically begin to challenge others' dreams. *Encourage* the dreamers, especially our Christian leaders. We must push them to claim what God has given them.

Two people are better off than one, for they can help each other succeed
Ecclesiastes 4:9
(New Living Translation)

Pastors preach, teach and they have visions. Even though you may not understand or share their dream or vision, you should encourage them to keep dreaming. Keep encouraging others to dream, and then your dream will also come true. In any case, don't let the dreams die. You don't always have to know another's dream in order to support them. We can just walk together and help keep their dream alive.

We are here only because our ancestors had dreams. We cannot let the dreams they had for us die. They did not want us to just stay content in whatever our current situations may be. Dreams are bigger than we are, and although we may not live to see them completed, we should always be a part of them. Blessed is a man who leaves a dream for his children. That dream is truly a vision.

Three weaknesses of mankind

We don't want to wait on God. Sometimes when we have a dream, we don't remain patient and dedicated because we want our dream fulfilled immediately in this culture of microwave Christianity. We want it now, with nothing unpleasant to endure. If you can't deal with rejection, pain, or disappointment, then you have no business receiving the miracle that God has for you. God should have this motto: If you have no pain with Me, you can't reign with Me.

We don't want to work to fulfill the dream. Nothing should stop a man or woman from working. Don't hold a grudge and make excuses—just find a job that needs to be done in the church or elsewhere. Stop taking personal holidays from church and calling in sick when ministries are developing. Too many church members call in sick on God and don't help grow His kingdom.

We have not changed our thinking pattern since the beginning of the stone age. Too many of us think we must physically use our hands rather than use our brains. It shouldn't matter if you work on a job or work on a ministry, you need to know that you can make your dream happen using your mind and heart. Go to the bible to learn to work the scripture. Work the Word.

We don't want to face war. The Lord says:

> *"And I have promised to bring you up
> out of our misery in Egypt into the land
> of the Canaanites, Hittites, Amorites,
> Perizzites, Hivites, and Jebusites, a
> land flowing with milk and honey."*
>
> Exodus 3:17 (New International Version)

As God helped the Israelites get out of Egypt, He did not lead them by the shorter path, which would involve fighting the Philistines. He told Moses:

> *"If they face war, they may change their
> minds and return to Egypt."*
>
> Exodus 13:17 (New International Version)

We are facing a new war. We need to return to being the priests of our own houses. Our power is not based on muscle or physical force . . . the war is not about suppression or prejudice. Focus on what you as an intelligent adult need to know about the world in order to seize control of your future. The economy is *global*, not local. Learn to understand economics and credit, learn how business works, and learn the intricacies of owning things. Don't sell out. Take responsibility.

You need to bring your tithes to the storehouse so we can take control through economic empowerment. There is a new war, and we need to enlist. The war is not just on the

Responsibility is the price of greatness.
—Winston Churchill

streets. This war affects us all, our families' futures and our churches' ministries.

Agreement to Reach Our Destiny

Agreement is designed to commit you to going the distance. Don't confuse the journey and the destination. Too many people think they have arrived and stop striving when they get married, or graduate, or get hired. That's just the beginning of the journey. Destiny begins once you pass the distance test. You must arrive at your agreed-upon destination before God releases more for you.

Agreement commits you to facing danger. We all need to have someone in agreement with us when we face danger. Ecclesiastes 4:12 teaches why two are better than one: Though one may be overpowered, two can defend themselves.

Agreement is also designed to move you into dominion. God wants man in agreement with Him to have dominion and to bear much fruit. For dominion to exist in our homes, there must be agreement between the heads of the family.

25

Harmony is pure love, for love is pure agreement.

–Lope de Vega

In 2011, the U.S. marriage rate was 6.8 marriages for every 1,000 citizens while the divorce rate was 3.6 per 1,000. That is more than half as many divorces as there are marriages. Because the heads of the family cannot come to agreement, we as a society have to deal with the plight of their troubled children.

Chapter Two

Breaking Strongholds

*P*atents protect unique ideas and inventions by putting up a wall to keep out everyone who would benefit from them—except, of course, those who license the patent and pay agreed-upon royalties. Patent holders don't hesitate to guard their property with vicious lawsuits.

Some companies are virtually tied up and trapped by their patents, putting their energy into defending their property rather than moving ahead to make the most of the opportunities their inventions offer. That is the downside of being barricaded in strongholds.

In a move that surprised many people in the technology world, Google and Samsung signed an agreement early in 2014 to share each other's patents for the next ten years. This will allow them to work together to research and develop new and future technologies and products and mine the wealth of all the patents they already own.

This agreement makes them stronger and gives them more protection from competitors, especially Apple. Apple has been fighting Samsung for years over Samsung's Android-based smartphones and tablets. It also guarantees that Samsung will continue to cooperate with Google even if it develops its own smartphone system.

Another benefit is that Google will be able to share the many patents it got when it bought Motorola for $12.5 billion in 2012; Samsung can use them in ways Google could not.

Samsung's Intellectual Property Center chief, Dr. Seungho Ahn, said, "This agreement with Google is highly significant for the technology industry. Samsung and Google are showing the rest of the industry that there is more to gain from cooperating than engaging in unnecessary patent disputes."

Google agreed. "We're pleased to enter into a cross-license with our partner Samsung," said Allen Lo, Deputy General Counsel for Patents at Google. "By working together on agreements like this, companies can reduce the potential for litigation and focus instead on innovation."

The Samsung-Google agreement is a great example of companies not allowing their strongholds to strangle creativity and cooperation. Instead of barricading themselves behind the walls of the patents, they worked out a harmonious, mutually beneficial agreement.

Strongholds protect but also destroy.

Strongholds are fortresses, castles, or walls, whether physical, emotional or spiritual. You normally think that a stronghold is just for protection, as when our God becomes a source of protection from physical as well as spiritual attacks:

> *The LORD is a refuge for the oppressed,*
> *a stronghold in times of trouble.*
>
> Psalm 9:10 (New International Version)

Strongholds are also walls built around our beliefs and emotions. Strongholds can be dangerous to our personal well-being, keeping us from healing and growing as they feed on our fear and strangle us. They prevent us from making the changes we need to make to grow in the kingdom. Strongholds prevent the truth of God's word from penetrating our hearts and minds so we will follow biblical principles and precepts for our lives.

Behold, You desire truth in the inward parts,

And in the hidden part You will make me to know wisdom.

Psalm 51:6 (New King James Version)

We're going to analyze both types of strongholds, looking at one we need to help build and protect, and some we need to tear down.

A stronghold against invaders is only as stalwart as its soldiers.

Let's study the rise and fall of the most famous physical stronghold ever built. Seven hundred years before Christ was born, Chinese emperors began to build a magnificent structure to protect their dynasties from invasion by the Mongol hordes to the north of China. It was built and rebuilt for over two thousand years. With all its branches, the wall is over 13,000 miles long, and it's the only man-made structure that can be seen from the moon. Over 25,000 watchtowers were built on the massive structure, and they were all manned with armed soldiers. Built to be the ultimate barrier, the wall cost an unimaginable amount of money, lives and effort.

Then one day the Manchu warriors bribed the commanding general, and he simply opened the gates and let in the enemy. After two thousand years, the stronghold became worthless as the enemy overran the kingdom.

The church should have a wall to protect the people and kingdom of God. Loyal troops should stand on the wall and man the guard towers, looking out to see the enemy coming from afar in order to alert the people of impending danger and perhaps forgo the destruction.

Ponder these questions:

"Are you in your assigned position on the wall? Or are you sleeping on duty, or have you even sold out the church?"

The church has faced the strongholds of persecution and oppression since its early inception. Opposition to the regenerative mind of Christ is a stronghold that continues to plague the church and prevent movement within the kingdom.

> *In those days when the number of disciples was increasing, the Grecian Jews among them complained against the Hebraic Jews because their widows were being overlooked in the daily*

distribution of food. So the Twelve gathered all the disciples together and said, "It would not be right for us to neglect the ministry of the word of God in order to wait on tables. Brothers, choose seven men from among you who are known to be full of the Spirit and wisdom. We will turn this responsibility over to them and will give our attention to prayer and the ministry of the word."

This proposal pleased the whole group. They chose Stephen, a man full of faith and of the Holy Spirit; also Philip, Procorus, Nicanor, Timon, Parmenas, and Nicolas from Antioch, a convert to Judaism. They presented these men to the apostles, who prayed and laid their hands on them.

So the word of God spread. The number of disciples in Jerusalem increased rapidly, and a large number of priests became obedient to the faith.

Acts 6:1-7 (New International Version)

God was establishing the new Church through a ministry of people who had been lost. Unfortunately, tyrannical spirits appear periodically, and they become unhappy about the progression of the church and its people.

We see in Acts 6 that as the church was growing, opposition and conflict arose between the Grecian Jews and the Hebraic Jews. The twelve disciples who manned the wall recognized the conflict as a destructive force that could hinder the progress of the church. With godly wisdom, they fortified the wall by appointing the first deacons in the church (verses 3-6). As a result, the church continued to flourish and the kingdom expanded.

Not only are we expected to sound the alarm when the walls are attacked, but we are expected to be a part of the solution, bring resolution, and offer a defense that will allow God's vision to continue.

Let's continue with the story of the new deacon, Stephen. He was an amazing deacon:

> *Now Stephen, a man full of God's grace and power, performed great wonders and signs among the people.*

The stronghold of ignorance and fear confronted his ministry. The establishment was afraid of change and tried to silence Stephen, and when they saw he was strong, wise and full of the Spirit, they lied about him, saying he was blaspheming. They brought in false witnesses, and ended up stoning him to death.

Meanwhile, the witnesses laid their clothes at the feet of a young man named Saul.

While they were stoning him, Stephen prayed, "Lord Jesus, receive my spirit." Then he fell on his knees and cried out, "Lord, do not hold this sin against them." When he had said this, he fell asleep.

And Saul was there, giving approval to his death.

On that day a great persecution broke out against the church at Jerusalem, and all except the apostles were scattered throughout Judea and Samaria. Godly men buried Stephen and mourned deeply for him. But Saul began to destroy the church. Going from house to house, he dragged off men and women and put them in prison.

Acts 6:8; 8:1-3 (New International Version)

This scripture prophetically speaks of a problem that has been ongoing for the 2,000 years since Stephen's time. These strongholds are the root of the continuous persecution--and sometimes even destruction--of the members of the body of Christ. These evil spirits show up and strategically attack us in our homes, at our churches, on our jobs, and in our schools. In fact, they strategically appear in most situations for the purpose of taking out leadership figures in order to increase the impact of persecution.

A stronghold is simply defined as a fortified place. Unfortunately, for the believer, strongholds become minatory [menacing] forces in their lives, making it difficult to have faith in our trying seasons and the inability to find rest in pleasant ones.

As soldiers of the kingdom, believers must take their posts on the wall and stand up to fight off the enemy, never selling out to the fleeting things of this world. Standing together, we must agree on one thing: We will always put the protection of the kingdom before our concerns for our individual churches, and we will break the stronghold that Satan has had on the kingdom for all these years.

The weapons we fight with are not the weapons of the world. On the contrary, they have divine power to demolish strongholds. We demolish arguments and every pretension that sets itself up against the knowledge of God, and we take captive every thought to make it obedient to Christ. And we will be ready to punish every act of disobedience, once your obedience is complete.

2 Corinthians 10:4-6 (New International Version)

The attack on the church.

If we look closely, we can identify the three elements involved in the attacks on the Church. Let's examine the tactics.

The Spirit of Saul. There is a Saul in your current church, someone who thinks he knows more about the church than the people of the church. Sauls attend services and participate in the church, but are not of the church. Sauls are typically negative and critical people, and their purpose is to destroy the church by driving people out and back into their houses, thus scattering the saints. Protectors of the wall should not allow this to happen. Major evangelism should take place to drive people to the church. Evangelists are the ones who can put Saul down when he approaches the wall.

The Spirit of Simon. Simon the sorcerer represents witchcraft. Simon types include gossipers, backstabbers, fortunetellers, emotionally unstable people, tricksters, and people who pray with crossed fingers. They may be baptized, but they have not received the Holy Spirit. They stubbornly refuse to submit to the authority of God or consult God for direction. Instead, they continue to do things their way. Simons also possess a spirit of Jezebel; they are manipulative, rebellious, and have an intense dislike for male authority. This spirit is very independent and extremely ambitious, glory seeking, and always looking for an avenue for self-aggrandizement. This spirit would rather destroy a person or an organization if it cannot control or dominate it.

Evangelism is not an option for Christians.

—Luis Palau

When Simon saw that the Spirit was given at the laying on of the apostles' hands, he offered them money and said, "Give me also this ability so that everyone on whom I lay my hands may receive the Holy Spirit." Peter answered: "May your money perish with you, because you thought you could buy the gift of

God with money! You have no part or share in this ministry, because your heart is not right before God. Repent of this wickedness and pray to the Lord in the hope that he may forgive you for having such a thought in your heart. For I see that you are full of bitterness and captive to sin."

Acts 8:18-23 (New International Version)

In addition to these strongholds being present in churches, schools, homes, and jobs, this spirit of Simon and Jezebel is running rampant in our communities. This spirit creates apparently harmless but distracting activities in the communities, at the schools, and on the job to limit your time at church or even pull you out of the church.

How can you pull down strongholds of Satan if you don't even have the strength to turn off your TV?
—Leonard Ravenhill

Inside the church, Simon's spirit stops you from becoming physically engaged in the service. His spirit hinders movement and the physical expression of praise and worship. As soldiers on the wall, we need to stand strong and confident that nothing and no one can curse what God has blessed.

As soldiers on the wall, we must not be afraid of these spirits. We must continue to serve, worship, and preach. When we man the wall, we provide a spiritual atmosphere within our churches where even the witches can be saved and transformed.

The devil's spirits. When we preach and worship, evil spirits should be forced out.

> *When the crowds heard Philip and saw the miraculous signs he did, they all paid close attention to what he said. With shrieks, evil spirits came out of many, and many paralytics and cripples were healed. So there was great joy in that city.*
>
> Acts 8:6-8 (New International Version)

Anytime the people of God have a close encounter with God, the devil wants to step in and stop the movement of God. Anytime the congregation is moving forward because people are being blessed, the devil will do whatever he can to stop their progress. Some struggle with sitting in services because they are afraid of the expressive movement of worship.

Remember, when God moves, even the strongest of men cry, and the hardest of women bow.

If you have never experienced the laying on of hands and the movement of the Holy Spirit, hesitate before you criticize. I have found that many people are too fond of misery. If that group includes you, I'm praying that you can break that stronghold by learning to celebrate God expressively.

The devil also wants to slow your spiritual movement—he wants to make your spirit stagnate. He knows if the people of God get together, we can change things. Every time you want to move forward or grow, the devil will trigger something in your life to make you stall and stagnate.

Learn to recognize the devil's tactics: All of a sudden, your feelings get in the way. Do you sometimes feel like you are going through hell, are in jail, or losing your mind? That's when you should get to the church regardless of how you feel. You're suffering from a stagnant spirit. Coming together in church will get the devil out of your spirit and your house. Don't miss another appointment with God!

Be on the lookout for sabotage–an 'inside job'. Those with camouflaged relationships with God, who make it look as though they are with you. Simon was baptized and joined the church. He camouflaged his relationship with God to look as though he was saved.

Declare today that you will not fake salvation! Rebuke those false spirits. ALL faking must stop.

God can deliver now. Strongholds are to be broken, not accepted.

Stop coming to church to be skeptical. Stop being the negative one in your group. Stop bringing others down.

> *Those who had been scattered preached*
> *the word wherever they went.*
>
> Acts 4:8 (New International Version)

The church must preach through the pressure. The apostles were persecuted and their followers were scattered far and wide, but they *all* continued to preach. Don't let folks stop you or discourage you from preaching. You must always have a word from the Lord.

When you're stressed, don't cuss your way out of the situation. *Preach* your way out of the situation and into better circumstances.

God's counterattack.

For every element the devil sends to attack the church, God sends an element to combat his attacks.

God will always prepare someone to take your place when you can no longer serve. God always has someone to take your place when you are out of place.

When Stephen was killed, God sent Philip, and he was not even a preacher, he was a deacon. Phillip had the Spirit of God on him and performed miraculous signs. You need to develop your own power and use the gifts God has given you to build the church. There should be more deacons out there standing on the wall and defending the faith. There ought to be members in the pews who can make a difference wherever they go. The preacher should not be the only one praying, healing and preaching. God has called all of us to fulfill the Great Commission. God's intent is that wherever we go on a daily basis, we work at His kingdom.

When Jesus came near, he spoke to them. He said, "All authority in heaven and on earth has been given to me. So wherever you go, make disciples of all nations: Baptize them in the name of the Father, and of the Son, and of the Holy Spirit. Teach them to do everything I have commanded you. "And remember that I am always with you until the end of time."

Matthew 28:18-20 (God's Word Translation)

Lay leaders should have the ground watered (prepared) whenever God has to send a pastor, prophet or evangelist. The pastor's job is to cast vision and preach the word, prepare you for fulfilling the mission of the church. Your job is to follow and allow the Holy Spirit to enlarge your gifts and abilities to win souls to the kingdom.

The Holy Spirit will bring freedom and deliverance from strongholds.

> *When the apostles in Jerusalem heard that Samaria had accepted the word of God, they sent Peter and John to Samaria. When they arrived, they prayed for the new believers there that they might receive the Holy Spirit, because the Holy Spirit had not yet come on any of them; they had simply been baptized in the name of the Lord Jesus. Then Peter and John placed their hands on them, and they received the Holy Spirit.*

Acts 8:14-17 (New International Version)

Prisons.

The bible says that Saul put the people in prison, in confinement (Acts 8:3). That was physical confinement, which the devil still does, but there are other kinds of prisons that are emotional or mental that the devil wants to imprison you in. If you don't confess and believe in Jesus Christ, you are in prison. If you lack joy, if you can't get Satan out of your house or your life, you are in prison. If you're bitter, oppressed, abused, or stuck in your past, then you are in prison. There are three prison systems:

Religious: Denomination pitted against denomination. Saul hated the new system, and he literally incarcerated the new believers. People are full of hate for other religions, even those which are similar. Wars are still being fought over religion.

Rebellious: When you remain ignorant, you don't see or try anything. You misinterpret things, don't act right, and reject authority.

Regional: Certain areas have regional problems or prejudices. We give our money to those who sacrifice it to their passions and misdirected missions. There are regional demonic spirits that keep you distracted by relatively unimportant issues instead of allowing you to focus on kingdom pursuits of dominion, prosperity, and prayer.

The church *must* provoke you—it *must* agitate you! And then you will change. Many come for comfort, friendship, a prayer, but we don't want a change. You can't break your stronghold unless you agitate the devil. Preach to the devil, and he will change.

You can't be afraid of the enemy! Stephen preached so hard it agitated the people to stone him to death (Acts 7:1-58). Stand on your feet with the Spirit of God filling your insides. A preacher should preach you to repentance and a desire for gladness and joy. Don't be afraid of the word of God; it will exalt you.

Some people are locked in their strongholds of knowledge, certain they know it all and never need to change. Never forget the bible is all about change.

> *All that you touch, You Change, All that you Change, Changes you. The only lasting truth is Change. God is Change.*
> —*Octavia E. Butler*

Moses told the Israelites they must be tired of living in Egypt and provoked them to leave.

Mordecai provoked Esther to change; he told her she was created for this time, but if she didn't go against the rules, God would put someone else in her place.

> *For if you remain silent at this time, relief and deliverance for the Jews will*

arise from another place, but you and
your father's family will perish. And who
knows but that you have come to your
royal position for such a time as this?"

Esther 4:14 (New International Version)

God called Jonah to visit a wicked city and preach to them that they were doomed, but Jonah was afraid and ran from them. After Jonah finally obeyed and preached the Word of God, the people changed and were saved.

Then Jesus came, stepped up, and provoked eternal change as the way of the truth and the light. Jesus said, "You must be born again."

It is not God's will nor his desire for you or the church to be in bondage to a stronghold.

On this rock I will build My church.
The powers of hell will not be able to
have power over My church.

Matthew 16:18 (New Life Version)

I will give you the keys of the kingdom
of heaven. Whatever you imprison,
God will imprison. And whatever you
set free, God will set free.

Matthew 16:19 (God's Word Translation)

Take your rightful place on the wall alongside the disciples! Protect the church as you also fight the strongholds within the kingdom.

Chapter Three

Are We One?

Business, Churches and the Kingdom

*P*ersonal relationships often drive even multi-billion-dollar business agreements. We're going to look at one of the biggest agreements ever made, where arrogance and lack of due diligence cost one company a prize and gave it to another.

In late 2013, Charter Communications was trying to buy Time Warner Cable in order to become a bigger player in the cable industry and compete with Comcast. Their bids were always "a day late and a dollar short," and were just above the actual stock value, sources said.

In addition to making nickel-and-dime bids, Charter insulted the Time Warner corporate leaders even more by trash-talking their management abilities. The New York Times talked to several people who gave insider views of what happened after

January 1, 2014, when Robert D. Marcus became CEO of Time Warner and decided to do more than just turn his cheek.

Mr. Marcus immediately and quietly contacted the CEO of Comcast, Brian L. Roberts, and suggested they talk about an agreement. Mr. Roberts actually played both sides for a while, also talking to Charter about making an alliance and getting some cable territories if Charter bought Time Warner. Comcast and Charter couldn't agree on how to take over Times Warner, and Mr. Roberts thought for awhile about not making any deal at all. When he met with his largest share-holders in February, though, they urged him to buy Time Warner. He had just bought NBC Universal in 2013, that deal had gone well, and the stock-holders were anxious to continue to grow. Mr. Roberts listened to them.

On his way to Russia, where his new acquisi-tion NBC was broadcasting the Olympics, Mr. Roberts called Mr. Marcus and committed to the deal. During the next few days, Mr. Roberts and Mr. Marcus were on the phone constantly, even during the Olympic opening ceremonies and a dinner with the International Olympic Committee. The due diligence and details were worked on by the management teams on both sides, who met in face-to-face conversations. The price was decided in a phone call between Mr. Roberts and Mr. Marcus--$45 billion dollars, all in stock. From start to end, the deal took 10 days.

Ironically, the day before they were ready to announce their monumental agreement, both companies were thrilled when Charter Communications had the arrogance to nominate a full slate of directors to Time Warner's board—the sign of a hostile take-over—without increasing its bid. "It created noise," one of the negotiators said. "We were able to do it under the cover of darkness."

The next day and without any advance notice to Charter Communications, Comcast subsidiary CNBC broke the news of the mega agreement.

Both company's boards approved the agreement immediately. Brian Robert's father, Ralph, said, "It was a very special moment." Ralph Roberts bought American Cable Systems in 1963, a small cable company that he renamed Comcast 45 years ago. He and his son grew the company to be the most powerful media company in America by making agreements of this type with other companies. They have always been conservative financially, and they don't take on lots of debt to expand.

By being united in their vision and goals for Comcast, Brian and Ralph Roberts were able to grow the company into a huge, profitable corporation. In this chapter, we discover how the power of One contributes to the growth of the kingdom, as we submit individually and corporately to the Holy Spirit. Let's establish the meaning of One as it relates both to the individual and the creation of a unit.

The number One.

Mathematically, One is always understood to be present even when it is not specifically defined or acknowledged. In algebraic equations, if no number is placed next to x, for example, it is understood that the x is really $1x$. This means if you multiply another number by x, it is assumed that you are multiplying that number by $1x$.

There are other important uses for the number One. In addition to One being the beginning of almost every numerical system, it is also referred to as an "empty product," which means One is also the result of multiplying no numbers at all.

Study the symmetry of the following mathematical equations involving the number one. We will use this chart to discuss how the elements of One relate to you.

1 x 1 = 1	1 + 1 = 2
1 x 1 x 1 = 1	1 + 1 + 1 = 3
1 x 1 x 1 x 1 = 1	1 + 1 + 1 + 1 = 4
1 x 1 x 1 x 1x 1 = 1	1 + 1 + 1 + 1 + 1 = 5

Did you see the pattern? One, by itself, multiplied by itself, only produces One--there is no growth. When unified Ones get together with other unified Ones and begin to multiply, there is growth. This chart demonstrates the numerical system on which all mathematics is based. As this formula is extended, you learn that it will always begin and end with One.

Even more intriguing, the number one represents the creation of a unified entity of two or more components. One married couple is the combination of a husband and a wife, for instance. One church is the sum of a pastor, elders, deacons and members of that congregation. This means that when two or more entities come together, they are re-identified as the one new entity that was created by their uniting.

To sum this all up, One is the absence of things, the beginning of things, the result of nothing, and the result of everything.

It's vital for you to understand the importance of One. After all, you are only one person. Understand your oneness, and see how powerful One really is.

The word of God says,

> *Just as a body, though one, has many*
> *parts, but all its many parts form one*
> *body, so it is with Christ. For we were*
> *all baptized by one Spirit so as to form*
> *one body—whether Jews or Gentiles,*
> *slave or free—and we were all given*
> *the one Spirit to drink.*
>
> 1 Corinthians 12:12-13 (New International Version)

I want you to have a biblical foundation as to why certain things are not working out for the good of God's people. Although 1 Corinthians teaches this, I often wonder, "Are we functioning as one body that was baptized by Jesus Christ?"

The goal of this chapter is to define a major factor in individuals' lives--the factor that affects their fractured relationships with themselves and with others, with their jobs, society, and the church. This chapter will require you to inventory your own spirit and the spirits of those with whom you regularly interact.

I pose the question *"are we One?"* because it is important to know if what someone says is truly what's in their spirit. Even further, do your words and actions match what God has placed in your spirit? Are you more concerned with presentation and appearances than you are with the spirit of things?

Often when we enter into relationships, we are too concerned with how many children she has or how much money he makes. Instead, we should be concerned about spiritual connections. For the sake of having a strong partner in times of trouble, we need to think in terms of how they would work as part of our single unit.

Looking into the spirit of things is a major question that has been asked in so many silent ways, even across our nation. When it comes to political decisions, Democrats, Republicans and independents challenge each other's beliefs and philosophies, sometimes bitterly. Whenever elected officials come to agreement and make solid, good decisions for the country or their town or state, the underlying spirit is more about their answering the public's question, "Are We One?" with a resounding "Yes!"

Moving on to the church, it is interesting how Paul's sermon in 1 Corinthians 12 talks about the body of the church and refers to it as *one*. The challenge of becoming one unit is discovering if we are all submitted to the same Christ. We are supposed to be functioning together as *one* within our churches. Instead, are we connected to members who are only part-time saved and halfway believers?

We expect God to do major works in our ministries and His kingdom, but we are not even sure of who is on our side in this battle. Too often we are in battle alongside people who pray with their fingers crossed, people who believe that the enemy is greater than us. These are the people we put on the front line!

Where there is unity, there is always victory.
—Publilius Syrus

The church is losing battles because many have come together without being *one* in faith, and they are not baptized in the spirit. To help you get to the place of Oneness, I would like to share several points for you to remember.

We are One when we focus on God's path.

All of our paths should lead to Heaven in spite of our many different callings and assignments. We lose Oneness because Heaven is not even a goal for many of us. We have not been truly convinced of what it takes to make it to heaven, so we have adopted the false belief that if we act like Christians or go to church every so often, we are on the right path. We emphasize our good deeds while we travel our own paths, not realizing how we oppose God's will for our lives and hinder the blessings of being in agreement with His will. This is why we have gigantic churches with thousands upon thousands of members and dead, worthless worship services.

It is a Path of Unity. In 1 Corinthians 12, Paul preaches about baptism of the body by the Spirit. Neither our human body nor our church body can exist as just a frame for what is on the surface; our mission is to look within.

> *For we were all baptized by one Spirit*
> *so as to form one body. v.13*

As we pursue relationships, we often fail to establish proper unity at the beginning. This is as true for an intimate relationship as it is for a church. We don't do what lawyers call "due diligence." We dive into quick commitments without looking beneath the superficial attraction, and to our chagrin—and pain—later we discover that we are not with the *One*. We were just hooked up or tied down, but we never had a proper unit. Just because people get together and present themselves as one does not mean they are a unit.

> *The hand of the* LORD *was upon me,*
> *and carried me out in the spirit of the*
> LORD, *and set me down in the midst of*
> *the valley which was full of bones,*

And caused me to pass by them round about: and, behold, there were very many in the open valley; and, lo, they were very dry.

And he said unto me, Son of man, can these bones live? And I answered, O Lord GOD, thou knowest.

Again he said unto me, Prophesy upon these bones, and say unto them, O ye dry bones, hear the word of the LORD.

Thus saith the Lord GOD unto these bones; Behold, I will cause breath to enter into you, and ye shall live:

Ezezekiel 37:1-5 (King James Version)

The body can be dead or alive; it can also be whole (complete), or empty. Some of us here on earth are whole while others are empty, and the status of the body will affect its ability to function as *one*. It must be understood that there are some "dry bones" among us, and the word of God must be spoken to them so that He can cause his "breath to enter into you, and ye shall live."

People and churches are dying because we can't

agree to speak to the dry bones. Instead we give up and bury them. God has established that there is hope for all. It is up to us to agree with Him and heal them with His spirit.

It is a Path of Diversity. We have discussed how one unit can—and should be—diverse. We in the body of Christ are unified but have tremendous diversity. One church will have people of different ages, backgrounds, gifts, wealth, commitment and insight. Diversity is extremely important for the development of the body and those of us who are a part of it.

The more diverse we are, the stronger a unit we become. The meshing of our differences allows us to thrive as One. There must be spontaneous movements in the body of Christ to ensure growth, and that begins with diversity, not disagreement. Consistency, not repetition, should be our goal. As humans, we thrive on spontaneity, and every now and then there should be some spontaneity in the body of Christ.

> *For Christians, who believe they are created in the image of God, it is the Godhead, diversity in unity and the three-in-oneness of God, which we and all creation reflect.*
>
> —Desmond Tutu

Diversity allows us to discover the truth about

each other—if that person is not who we thought we were married to, if the person sharing our pew is crossing his fingers.

It is a Path of Uniqueness. One successful church is not a copy of another. You can only be good at what you are and not what someone else is. We are not the same. Your qualities are unique and valuable. The challenge, however, is getting everyone to accept and understand this value in order to get together as one on the right path. Being unique means you possess a quality that indicates you are qualified for whatever God plans for you, as others are qualified for whatever God plans for them.

The challenge is in getting everyone to function as a diverse body with many members while we are as one in Christ. We can look unified, we can be diversified, we can have quality, but we might not be going down the path together. As Christians, we must make sure that we follow Christ's mission and actively seek disciples.

Some of us within the church attend but are not authentic followers of Christ. We may look and act saved, but when it is just a false front, our spirits fester and rot, contaminating and endangering the rest of the unit.

As part of a unit, we infect all those with whom

we're in agreement. Infection is a systemic process. We need to infect our unit with the Holy Spirit, not with our falsity.

Shouting "hallelujah!" does not save you! Too many of us are more concerned with being members than with being saved. God's purpose is to fill us with the Holy Spirit and put us into a closer relationship with Him; then we can all walk on one path. All of us are gifted with something, and no one should strive to dominate the functioning of the body. Our title and position within the unit do not matter. What *does* matter is if you help the unit stay on the path.

> *"I have sworn, and I will perform it, that*
> *I will keep thy righteous judgments."*
>
> Psalms 119:106 (King James Version)

I keep mentioning that we all must be on one path, and that all paths should lead to heaven. Now I would also like to add that Christ is our word and our path.

> *The Word became flesh and made his*
> *dwelling among us. We have seen his*
> *glory, the glory of the one and only Son,*
> *who came from the Father, full of grace*
> *and truth.*
>
> John 1:14 (New International Version)

This is why dedicating yourself to bible study and developing a personal relationship with Him are so important. The challenge of intimacy with God—having close encounters with Him—is far more demanding than coming to church once a week. It's about creating a sincere, authentic relationship with Jesus. It's essential that you commit to bible study and discipleship classes for personal growth and to understand where God is moving individually and corporately. You can't get that with one or two hours on Sundays. You can't establish a life of ministry or faith when it's not part of your public life.

The more you continue to read Scripture, the more you begin to think as He thinks and act as He acts. And that's how, over time, you gain the wisdom of the ages.
—Wayne Cordeiro, The Divine Mentor

When the spirit of God does not live in us, there is no unity. Instead, we're confused and dysfunctional. Understand this: The church needs everyone to study the Word of God. So why do we resist? We have many excuses that keep us from studying the Bible. We prevent ourselves from receiving the scriptural teaching that helps us overcome the many challenges we face.

We need to stop wasting time attacking one another and being skeptical of those trying to be a blessing to us—church against church, denomination against denomination, pastor against pastor. Of course, these are not all of the challenges that face the church.

Christ's mission was to heal people in every area of their lives, and we should follow in His footsteps.

We should deliver people from insecurities and low self esteem instead of adding to their burdens. We need to start embracing diversity and the differences among us, accept people for who they are and start dealing with the inner man instead of what is on the surface.

We need to bless others and not attack them.

A philosophy of excellence.

Each person fulfilling his or her duties to the utmost can generate great power when gathered together, and a chain of such power can generate a ring of power. (Kiichiro Toyoda, at the dedication of the first Toyota Motor Co. plant, November 1937)

Toyota Motor Company introduced the well-made, economical Corolla to American car buyers in 1966, 30 years after building their first Model AA car in Japan. In an era ruled by muscle cars, V-8 engines and cheap gas, the little Corolla became an instant hit with Americans. By the 1970s, Toyota was the best-selling import brand. During the 1980s, they started to manufacture vehicles in the U.S. via an agreement with General Motors. Today, Toyota continues to earn top honors for product quality.

When Toyota came on the scene, the Ford Motor Company was the premier automobile maker based in America. What made Toyota so successful is that their marketers never focused on attacking Ford. Instead, their strategy was to build the best possible car and allow the consumers to choose. The company valued the efforts of their workers, and had a philosophy of excellence.

If each person makes the most sincere effort in his assigned position, the entire company can achieve great things.
—Kiichiro Toyoda, 2002

In the church, God is the consumer making a decision about who's ready for Him. He's not interested in lip service about how right we are and how wrong others are. He's just looking for the best products, those who focus on what He desires from them, those who focus on tailoring themselves to meet the needs of the ministry. God checks and tests the church's products that we display.

The church today is dysfunctional, although we are unified with our activities and routines. We are dysfunctional because when it comes to real spiritual growth, wholeness and completeness in God, we are all over the page—we are not One. We have all types of motives, and some are divisive and out of control. God says to the church, "At some point you must grow up enough for the body to function properly and true growth to begin."

> *Then we will no longer be infants, tossed back and forth by the waves, and blown here and there by every wind of teaching and by the cunning and craftiness of people in their deceitful scheming.*
>
> *Instead, speaking the truth in love, we will grow to become in every respect the mature body of him who is the head, that is, Christ.*
>
> *From him the whole body, joined and held together by every supporting ligament, grows and builds itself up in love, as each part does its work.*
>
> Ephesians 4:14-16 (New International Version)

When we mature and grow with a clear vision and purpose, believers will not focus on pettiness, or on the personalities or weaknesses of other members. Instead they will "speak the truth in love" and anoint the lives of all those who work in ministry. In the church we must learn and teach the truth about having a relationship with Jesus and the Word of God.

When a man operates in unity with God, his whole life—his finances, his family, his career—will line up with God's plan, because finally his house is in order. God is a God of order, and He blesses what He orders.

Another part of having a relationship with God is the unselfish act of tithing. On Mt. Sinai, God gave Moses many commands and agreements. Tithing was the last, but it was not the least:

> *"A tithe of everything from the land, whether grain from the soil or fruit from the trees, belongs to the LORD; IT IS HOLY TO THE LORD."*
>
> Leviticus 27:30 (New International Version)

The body of Christ must stop talking about why we can't tithe! This is an agreement that we have made with God.

> *"Ever since the time of your ancestors you have turned away from my decrees and have not kept them. Return to me, and I will return to you," says the LORD Almighty.*
>
> *"But you ask, 'How are we to return?'*

"Will a mere mortal rob God? Yet you rob me.

"But you ask, 'How are we robbing you?'

"In tithes and offerings. You are under a curse—your whole nation—because you are robbing me. Bring the whole tithe into the storehouse, that there may be food in my house. Test me in this," says the LORD Almighty, "and see if I will not throw open the floodgates of heaven and pour out so much blessing that there will not be room enough to store it."

Malachi 3:7-10 (New International Version)

Divisiveness is not diversity. It is an enemy, and it has affected more than the church. Along with selfishness, it's also affected the family—husband against wife, wife against husband, brother against brother and sister against sister.

Jesus knew their thoughts and said to them, "Every kingdom divided against itself will be ruined, and every city or household divided against itself will not stand."

Matthew 12:25 (New International Version)

Think of the power of agreement, the strength when there's agreement among the heads of the family. Women, we need you to stop beating up your husband and acting like Job's wife. God has called you to be a helpmate, not a hatemate, and your charge is to support that man no matter what. Be there for him at his time of need and *especially* during sickness and hard times. If he believes in God's miracles and you speak against God, your house is now divided.

A house divided against itself cannot stand.
—Abraham Lincoln

Satan tested Job to see if he would curse the Lord. After destroying everything Job had and killing his children, Satan gave him painful sores all over his body. It's important to remember how Job and his wife handled this test:

> *And he took a piece of broken pottery with which to scrape himself, and he sat [down] among the ashes.*

> *Then his wife said to him, Do you still hold fast your blameless uprightness? Renounce God and die!*

> *But he said to her, You speak as one of the impious and foolish women would speak. What? Shall we accept [only]*

68

good at the hand of God and shall we
not accept [also] misfortune and what
is of a bad nature? In [spite of] all this,
Job did not sin with his lips.

Job 2:8-10 (Amplified Bible)

The Path Leads to the Kingdom.

Jesus talks about the kingdom, and this is what your house should be concerned with. If your only focus is on your physical house—your four walls and no more—it is already divided against itself.

When people study this scripture and discuss Job and his wife, most tend to zone in on the husband and wife aspect. The issue really is the kingdom and God's will being done on earth. Job understood this, and he knew the issue was bigger than he was. That is why after all Satan's tests and all Job's suffering, he rebuked his wife when she told him to curse God—without abusing or beating her, because that would be a sin.

Job did not side with his wife to create peace in his home. Job thought of the Kingdom first, and handled her accordingly. Even though he didn't know God gave Satan permission to challenge him, he still knew that God would not forsake him.

The devil does not want you to understand that

the kingdom rules. If Satan can get you to focus on non-kingdom stuff, he keeps you enslaved and you don't even know it. If we become part of God's kingdom and don't worry about just our own house being blessed but about someone else's house being blessed as well, we can be elevated.

Notice that Jesus mentioned that the city can be divided, too, telling us that the city must be in agreement as well. If the entire body of Christ starts praying for the kingdom, then the city will change and in return we will have a blessed effect on our houses.

Christians should be in prayer for the church, the city, the community, and our country. We cannot pray for only our own family, needs and belongings. If we put the kingdom first, our homes will automatically be blessed.

Focus on God's Presence.

Many Christians pray for cars, houses, jobs and spouses, but we neglect to pray for God's presence.

When the children of Israel left their place of bondage in Egypt, God was with them. He guided them and lit their way:

> *By day the LORD went ahead of them*
> *in a pillar of cloud to guide them on*
> *their way and by night in a pillar of*

fire to give them light, so that they could travel by day or night. Neither the pillar of cloud by day nor the pillar of fire by night left its place in front of the people."

Exodus 13:21-22 (New International Version)

The sun shall not smite thee by day, nor the moon by night."

Psalms 121:6 (King James Version)

There are two symbols of God's presence here— the cloud and the fire. The lesson is that if the people of God can focus more on receiving God's presence rather than on money, things, and being distracted by annoying people, His favor will come. As a person of God, especially as a leader, you should always desire and need to be in a position where God's presence is with you.

God's presence confirms His agreement with us. God is always present because He is omnipresent. However, there are strategic times in ministry movements, family, and business when you must ask God for His presence. This will make you assured, confident, and clear on assignments and victory.

Throughout the Bible, there are examples of man asking for His presence. Gideon asked for it (Judges

6:16-39), and David asked for it (Psalms 51:11). Thomas asked to see Jesus' hands (John 20:24-25). It is all right to ask.

> *"Then Moses said to him, "If your Presence does not go with us, do not send us up from here. How will anyone know that you are pleased with me and with your people unless you go with us? What else will distinguish me and your people from all the other people on the face of the earth?"*
>
> *And the LORD said to Moses, "I will do the very thing you have asked, because I am pleased with you and I know you by name."*
>
> Exodus 33:15-17 (New International Version)

At this point in the story of Moses and the exodus of the children of Israel, the people were closer to the Promised Land than they had ever been. Unfortunately, they were all frustrated, and Moses was weary. God had not shown him signs to make him feel comfortable. Still, Moses didn't ask God to make the situation better. Instead Moses asked God for His presence. He knew God's presence was necessary not only for victory, but to tell others that the Israelites were truly "set apart."

Too many Christians proclaim salvation and victory without ever being concerned about His presence.

The term *presence* means to be above, to be over, to go before, to be within, or to fight for. God's presence guarantees your success more than just giving you the things *you* think you need to succeed. Personally, I want God's presence and agreement all around me so that when people see me coming, they will see the power of agreement He and I have.

We should ask for God's presence rather than God's presents. We need to get out of the car and house business, the spouse and money business and into the presence business. If we do, Oneness and victory are sure to happen.

Our prayers should begin, "Lord, how will they know you are going to fix my credit unless they sense your presence with me?" or "How will they believe in healing if your presence is not with me?" or "How do I keep my daughter safe from danger and out of someone's bed unless you go with her?"

If a church doesn't seek the presence of God, when the world visits their sanctuary, they will not see *one* body in agreement. They will see a splintered church, with one group dead, one group fighting, and only a fraction worshiping. We need to start praying for God's presence because when He shows up, He is unmistakable.

Paul indicates that the presence of God's spirit is by baptism:

> For we were all baptized by one Spirit so as to form one body—whether Jews or Gentiles, slave or free—and we were all given the one Spirit to drink.
>
> 1 Corinthians 12:13 (New International Version)

Matthew 3:11 explains baptism as a twofold process. We can't move as a body until we know that everyone is baptized not just by water but also by the fire:

> "I baptize you with water for repentance. But after me comes one who is more powerful than I, whose sandals I am not worthy to carry. He will baptize you with the Holy Spirit and fire.
>
> Matthew 3:11 (New International Version)

Jesus didn't need to be baptized by the fire because He *was* the fire. Christ didn't have to repent because

He never sinned. Most of us have repented and been baptized, and that's good, but we're not *one* with Him. We lack the Spirit—the second baptism with the Holy Spirit and fire—which is why we lack the power of God. Being baptized by the Spirit is not just about speaking in tongues.

> *When the day of Pentecost came, they were all together in one place. Suddenly a sound like the blowing of a violent wind came from heaven and filled the whole house where they were sitting. They saw what seemed to be tongues of fire that separated and came to rest on each of them. All of them were filled with the Holy Spirit and began to speak in other tongues as the Spirit enabled them.*
>
> Acts 2: 1-4 (New International Version)

The bible specifically points out that the apostles and others were all together in one place, in one accord, and in agreement. They were one in spirit, all waiting on the same thing, the thing that Jesus had promised them before his ascension.

This is so important! If only a few were waiting while the others doubted, I do not believe they would have received this historic move of God.

Too many of us are in social circles; we gather together and even dine together, but because we are not spiritually waiting on the same things, we never receive the Holy Spirit. Agreement and Oneness are this important. All of us are not waiting on the Spirit; some of us are waiting on supplies, resources, and spouses when we really should be waiting on the Holy Ghost to show up.

From this scripture, I know that His fire is available to all who desire it, especially when "two or three gather in his name" (Matthew 18:20). Fire identifies who has been saved. Because fire purifies and cleanses us, it makes me wonder why some people do not want to be touched by it.

Some of us don't even want to be hugged or touched by people full of God's fire. Since when did that become a bad thing? The church in Acts 2 and Jesus' promises in Acts 1 prove its necessity. Our inability to come in agreement on this issue is hindering the kingdom and destroying households. Even when people don't speak in tongues, their lives should represent cleanliness and freeness.

To reject the spirit of God is to reject the desire to be in His presence. People need to understand that the fire allows you the privilege of sitting in the presence of God in your imperfect state. He works on you and stops your struggles from holding you back. If you are still trapped by your stronghold of beliefs and struggle at the presence of God, then you need a touch so that you may be cleansed and stand in agreement with the body of Christ.

When we all are baptized in the Spirit, it displays unity, power, and the agreement that Christ is in control. The gift of tongues, although unique to each individual, shows unity and power and assurance from God that it is good that we strive, and it's all right if we don't get it right all the time.

We need to free ourselves from traditions and other strongholds and start asking God to fill us with His power, with His Spirit, and with His love. Even with the gift of tongues, if we do not have His power, love and spirit, we cannot resist the enemy as he tries to divide the body of Christ.

When we ask for God's presence, we should ask for a Pentecostal movement-- not the denomination, but the touch of fire.

I want to point out another thing regarding the presence of God and the Holy Spirit: The Holy Spirit infuses the entire body of Christ. As it is imparted to you, evil spirits are loosed from the midst and bound in hell.

All persons, not just church leaders, must be filled, and the entire body needs to possess the spirit of the Living God.

God's Spirit is the power we need to overcome the challenges that undermine our commitment to Him and allows us to operate in our diversity as One.

Chapter Four

What Is Commitment?

*T*raditionally, when a large European or American company partners with an African company, the agreement isn't the fairest. The African company supplies raw ingredients at a price determined by the large company, and that's it. The company buying the ingredients has little concern about sustainability, damage to the environment, or a living wage for the people who harvested, manufactured, or created the product. There's not a commitment or a true partnership.

The consumers usually have no idea of the fairness of the agreements and commitments that have been made in the creation of the final products when they purchase them. Traditionally, they did not care.

That's beginning to change, especially in the cosmetic business. Some ingredients from Africa are superior to any found anywhere else in the world, and they're in hot demand. Policies and protocols are being established to protect the African environment, workers and entrepreneurs; fair trade and "fair wild" policies are more common every day.

"Fair wild ensures that the crop is being both fairly traded and sustainably harvested," according to Susan Curtis, director of natural health at Neal's Yard, a cosmetics company in London. Neal's Yard buys frankincense from Kenya.

The New York Times wrote an article about how argan oil from Morocco created huge interest in many exceptional African natural products. Clarins, Patyka, and Colbert M.D. use several "exotic" oils in their $85-$125 moisturizers.

Even more exciting, some companies are actually partnering with African entrepreneurs. Kanshi is a new line of aromatherapy and body care products that will be introduced in 2014; it's owned jointly by Dzigbordi Dosoo of Ghana and a New Jersey skin care line.

A British company, Lush, buys its shea butter from a women's collective in Ghana; they created a YouTube video about the 400 women in the collective. L'Occitane en Provence received an award from the United Nations for the work it did in Burkina Faso.

Magatte Wade is a New York store owner

originally from Senegal. She created Tiossan, a line of bath products and fragrances using traditional Senegalese healing ingredients, and she plans to move her manufacturing plant to Senegal.

A Nielsen study showed that 44% of Americans are willing to pay more for products that come from companies committed to being socially responsible. This is a recent phenomenon, and the number of consumers feeling this way is growing very fast—up almost 25% from 2011 to 2013.

When people buy fair trade or fair wild products, or buy from a socially responsible manufacturer, they make a commitment to those who agree to do what's right.

Let's discover how the principle of commitment is necessary for success, in corporations, families, and the church.

> *Commit to the Lord whatever you do, and He will establish your plans.*
>
> Proverbs 16:3 (New International Version)

> *Commit thy works unto the LORD, and thy thoughts shall be established.*
>
> Proverbs 16:3 (King James Version)

*Roll your works upon the Lord [commit
and trust them wholly to Him; He will
cause your thoughts to become agreeable
to His will, and] so shall your plans be
established and succeed.*

Proverbs 16:3 (Amplified Bible)

What is commitment?

First, commitment is an agreement. It's also a
promise, a contract. I believe we can agree that the
word *commitment* is not a popular term in our society
today. Commitment seems to mean "one-way" to
more people each year.

Let's look at the economic structure. Corporate
America wants you to commit to aligning your life to
its mission and goals. However, corporate America is
not equally committed to you. When your boss says
that he is hiring you because of your resume or your
qualifications, he wants you to come in and commit
to the company, put in forty to sixty hours a week
and short-change your family.

A company often used to promise the security of
a lifelong job if you put them first and worked hard.
Yet today the first step most companies make when
things are tough is to reduce staff costs—to eliminate
your benefits, or let you go, or hire people from a

temporary agency. You change from a corporate asset to a corporate liability. You feel like your commitment and trust have been violated.

We can turn the tables and ask about the commitment you make to your employer, too. As an employee, do you always hold up your side of the agreement? Do you spend your time on your cell phone or on Facebook instead of doing your tasks? Do you go in with a clear mind—not tired or hung over—and give them your best self? Or do you hold back, and go through the motions? Are you dedicated to achieving the company's goals, or of increasing your value to the company by increasing productivity and creativity while at the same time decreasing costs?

The best way to appreciate your job is to imagine yourself without one.
—Oscar Wilde

Let's look at relationships. Many people believe there is no such thing as "real marriage." It does not matter whether you are saved or unsaved; statistics show your marriages are not lasting. Marriage is on the decline. For some reason, the soft glow of the honeymoon turns into a raging thunderstorm. The bolts and sparks cause confusion, anger and conflict. Well before all the options are discussed and considered, someone—whether it's the woman or the man—decides this relationship is too much work and pain, and they go their separate ways.

If you are not married, we know your status is even more precarious. How long can you hang onto your man or woman? How committed is their love? Or will they even commit to saying what they feel is "love?"

When your sweetheart doesn't answer your text or call back right away, suspicion sets in. Pretty soon you doubt their commitment, and you might even try to beat them to the breakup so you're not the one who's dumped. Lord help them if they lose a job; they become the liability instead of the asset.

Let's look at churches. Now this lack of commitment has moved from corporate America, to the employee, to intimate relationships (whether you are married, single, or independent), and now it is trickling into the church. There is a growing lack of commitment to the kingdom. Do you recognize any of these excuses?

"I come on the first and third Sunday; you should be happy I am here because I have to cut the yard and take care of weekend chores."

"My family needs me so I can't give God that much time."

"I'm saved, and I'm in the church so I owe God nothing."

"I'll just keep praying, and He will keep answering."

"I don't have to be in a ministry."

"I don't have to go to class; I've studied the Bible before."

"As a matter of fact, I did pray for my job, but now that I have the job, I don't go to church anymore."

"I don't give like I used to because I've given *so* much."

"When I was in a desperate situation, you could not keep me off the altar. You could not keep me from God's house, but now I have caught up with my house payment, and my house is in order. I paid off two of my ten credit cards."

"I am not coming, and I don't care what you say today. I'm still not going to do it, because you are just trying to get me to be a part of your ministry."

Commit to the Lord whatever you do and he will establish your plans.

Say "commit." Commit your works to the Lord, and your thoughts will be established.

Jesus says,

> *"I am the way and the truth and*
> *the life. No one comes to the Father*
> *except through me."*

John 14:6 (New International Version)

You can't come to Him on my shirttails, or your father's, or your mother's prayers. Jesus says, "You have to come through me."

Too often we are looking for affirmation from people, when we should be looking for affirmation from God..

Forget all the material things; you can't come through the Father for happiness if you don't know Him. Through this process and through this arena, we all wrestle with commitment at some time or other.

You may say, "Why should I be committed when I spent forty to fifty hours at work this week? Then I had to spend hours with my children, and now my spouse is asking for a family day?" The Proverbs scripture explains why the believer should commit to the Lord *whatever* he or she does. The question is, are we committing our works to the Lord? As we look closer at this verse, several things become evident to us.

The process of discovery will lead you to a vision and vision path.

This is the process of *discovery*. Commitment in this context says commit to the Lord, and it tells us you have to go through the discovery process of being brutally honest with yourself where your loyalties and allegiance lies.

Ask yourself: *Am I committed to the Lord for my job, my family, my future?* Are you? To whom are you really committed? With the process of discovery, we go through a two-fold challenge.

We first *learn to be committed* to someone. We have a family in our church, Oscar and his wife, Soweto, who have some smart, handsome children; the boys look just like their father. The children's first level of commitment is to their mama—their first word, their first love. From an early age until they leave the house, their commitment is to their mother and grows to include their father, both of them loving parents who meet their needs and cherish them.

As adult believers, our dependency for provision and care should come from our relationship with God through Jesus Christ. Children, on the other hand, only know that their father and mother are who takes care of them and their every need. Unfortunately, some of us are still at the childhood stage, still depending on mama and daddy. We walk into church and declare that we have a relationship with the Lord, but we are not really committed to Him.

As children grow through the years, if the adults aren't committed to each other and to the children, there will be conflict. If there is no agreement between the family members on common goals and vision for the family, there will be conflict. Single parents can have conflict in the household, too. Maybe a man claims he is a father or steps in as stepfather but is not totally committed to the care of the children as well as the mother. The lower their level of commitment, the more conflict there will be. How can children learn to commit if no one commits to them?

The process of discovery not only affects the children but it affects their parents, because these parents *must* be committed to them. Why bring a child into the world if you are not going to commit to them? If you are the father, be a father, not an absentee parent. If you must be absent, your obligations don't leave the house when you leave. . . you *must* still send a check . . . you *must* still maintain a loving relationship with your children.

And remember that fathers need commitment too. Daddy knows how the children got here, and he had some help during seedtime and harvest. Don't put the entire burden on him. There are so many demands in a family, so much is going on, and it can become fertile ground for conflict. Parents have their own needs, and the children have their needs, and the Lord requires unity and alignment within the family and with him.

Let's return to Oscar's situation as father and head of the household. The pastor says, "You have to be at church on Sunday, and you need to be in a ministry." Oscar is tired. *Commit to the Lord whatever you do.* One conflict is that many of us commit more to a person than we do to God. All of a sudden on a Sunday morning, the pastor asks Oscar to stand and shout "Praise God" and bless the name of Jesus. But the only name Oscar can think of is Soweto ("that's who I've been with all week, and she's been calling my name"). And all he hears is, "Daddy, I need shoes, Daddy, I need your time and love and attention!"

Now the pastor is saying that God is sending us to another level, another direction, and Oscar asks, "Why do I have to commit?" First you should know that you are not committing to your pastor as much as you are committing to the Lord. Commit to the Lord whatever you, do and your plans will succeed.

Our lives are complicated by the layers of commitments we must make. Not only are a husband and wife like Oscar and Soweto committed to the Lord, to each other and to their sons, they have to wrestle with the mundane and demanding day-to-day commitments as parents. Soweto and Oscar have to have jobs to put food on the table, put shoes on their boys' feet and jeans on their legs, and save for vacations and college educations.

Oscar and Soweto have to work diligently to stay focused on their jobs, but the jobs are not equally committed to them. If they call in sick too many times, they're fired. When Christ says, "I am the way, the truth, and the life," the pastor is trying to teach Oscar the level of trust and agreement to biblical principles God requires as he discovers this process.

You don't choose your family. They are God's gift to you, as you are to them.
—Desmond Tutu

What does Oscar do on a Sunday morning when his intentions are good, he plans to get up and go to the Lord's house, but his car won't start? Has he been putting too much thought on his possessions, his car, and his family? Does his commitment motivate him to find another way of getting to church? Or does he say, "Guess it's a sign; I need to sleep in."

Let's continue the process of discovery by studying Proverbs 16:3 some more. The text says to commit to the Lord whatever you do, or commit your works to the Lord. The New International Bible says about our "plans," and the King James Version says "thoughts." The Amplified Bible, in its detailed explanation, includes both. All three versions explain that when we commit to someone or something, our minds remain focused on the object of our commitment.

So when you have put your hopes and commitments in a car that breaks down, or to a man or woman who deserts you, your thoughts and plans go to waste.

Simply put, the scripture says: "Commit to the *Lord.*" He will take care of you. Your plans will succeed, and your thoughts will succeed.

The Lord also wants you to know you will have burdens when you are putting too much thought on people and things, and not on Him. Many of us are carrying burdens we don't need. Heavy burdens weaken relationships and commitments; they cause brokenness. In all relationships, when we are not wholly committed to each other, someone has to separate—it leads to brokenness.

When a husband gives his wife 100 percent, but she gives only 50 percent because she's burdened, the marriage won't last long. Brokenness! Is she giving 100 percent but his burdens prevent him from giving more than 75 percent? Their relationship won't last long. Brokenness.

Give your burdens to the LORD, and he will take care of you. He will not permit the godly to slip and fall.
—Psalm 55:22
(New Living Translation)

When a mother tries to take care of her son, but he thinks he is grown and doesn't want to abide by her rules, doesn't have a job, is still driving on Mom's gas but still wants to talk back to her, there's no commitment from him. He's a burden to her, and that will weaken *her* commitment. His burdens cause brokenness.

Commit to the Lord whatever you do and your plans will succeed.

How can you pray for a raise when you have never tithed? You believe that God should bless you since you were saved, but God says you have never been committed to Him. So now you are in God's house, you have been tithing for about three months but the last seven years you did not tithe. Do you think the last three months wiped out your long-term lack of commitment?

After we realize it is a process of discovery, we need to *accept it means doing the work God assigned us to do*. Do you see yourself as you really are? Have you fulfilled all your commitments? Are you serving in your local church as God has assigned you, based on your gifts, ability, passion and experience?

If you are honest with yourself when you answer these questions, you are in the process of discovery. God gifted each of us with special skills when we became kingdom dwellers so we could perform a unique service to the church. By using our individual skill sets, we bring glory to God by completing our assignment in the kingdom.

Jesus said,

> *"I have brought you glory on earth by completing the work you gave me to do."*
>
> John 17:4 (New International Version)

Jesus recognized His agreement with God concerning His assignment here on earth. As Jesus committed Himself to complete His work, He brought glory to God.

Our commitment to God is just as important. When we come into agreement with the Father and fulfill our assignment for Him here on earth, we too bring glory to His name!

Chapter Five

The Issue with Commitment

Pressing On

Commitment takes many forms, as we'll discuss in this chapter. Business commitments are very hard to keep straight; there are layers of agreements and commitments piled on top of each other in every business deal. Loyalties can change in a heartbeat, and those at the top can get canned as quickly as those at the bottom.

George Zimmer founded Men's Wearhouse in Houston in 1973, when he sold $25 polyester sport coats out of his van and used a cigar box as a cash register. Over the years he made good decisions and built his one-van operation into a publicly traded men's clothing business worth well over $2 billion. He was known as a progressive and liberal business owner.

In 2011, Mr. Zimmer handpicked his successor as CEO and moved on to become chairman of the board. However, he quickly lost faith in his choice, Mr. Ewert, for giving huge pay increases to himself and other executives, selling off parts of the company, and making other decisions over Mr. Zimmer's protests.

After talking with some investment bankers in April, 2013, Mr. Zimmer decided to make an attempt to take Men's Wearhouse private and regain some of his influence. Two months later, he brought the idea to his board, and Mr. Ewert promptly pressured the board to fire Mr. Zimmer.

After watching the fireworks in the Men's Wearhouse boardroom, the investment bankers licked their chops and contacted another client of theirs, Jos. A. Banks, a smaller men's clothing firm. The two companies had been bitter rivals for years, always trying to undercut each other on price. The bankers suggested that Jos A. Banks make a $2.3 billion-dollar purchase of Men's Wearhouse.

Men's Wearhouse refused the bid and tried to swallow a poison pill—buying another company that would increase their debt load. Bankers started pressuring Men's Wearhouse to cooperate, consider the offer, and even open their books for review, but they refused.

Less than two weeks later, Men's Wearhouse

turned the tables on Jos. A. Banks and offered $1.5 billion for *their* company. This is called the Pac-Man defense, when prey turns predator. When the offer was refused, Men's Wearhouse raised its bid to $1.6 billion and "went hostile," threatening to nominate new board members to Jos A. Banks' board.

The bankers suddenly switched sides, urging Jos. A. Banks to cooperate and open *their* books, but Jos. A. Banks decided to swallow its own poison pill, agreeing to buy Eddie Bauer from a private equity company.

Finally, Men's Wearhouse raised its bid to almost $1.8 billion—and the Jos. A. Banks' board became interested. The companies met to talk over a busy weekend. In March 2014, the bid was finally increased to a full $1.8 billion, the deal was cut—and Eddie Bauer was dumped (though it will get a $48 million penalty fee).

Men may not always keep their agreements with you, but God does. With Him, it is a done deal.

The new clothing company will have revenue of $3.5 billion per year. Like many newly merged companies, the first thing it will do is lay off marketing, customer service, warehouse and purchasing personnel to save money, to the tune of $100 million per year.

Also left behind was George Zimmer, the founder of this small empire. In an interview in Fortune Magazine, he said his time had come and gone.

When it comes to commitment, there are many challenges that must be overcome to reach a point of agreement. Commitment inspires us to persevere through challenges, obstacles, and setbacks in order to make the sacrifices necessary to reach agreement. Commitment pushes us to become creative, to push the limits, to resolve the challenges that lead to agreement. If The Men's Wearhouse had not continued to push the limit, and become creative in their challenges, an agreement would not have been reached. One that extended the market and corporate vision. Let's look at how the Bible encourages us to approach commitment and challenges.

Not that I have already obtained all this, or have already arrived at my goal, but I press on to take hold of that for which Christ Jesus took hold of me. Brothers and sisters, I do not consider myself yet to have taken hold of it. But one thing I do: Forgetting what is behind and straining toward what is ahead, I press on toward the goal to win the prize for

*which God has called me heavenward
in Christ Jesus.*

Following Paul's Example

*All of us, then, who are mature should
take such a view of things. And if on
some point you think differently, that
too God will make clear to you.*

Philippians 3:12-15 (New International Version)

I love this scripture; Paul shares with us that he
is pressing on for a prize: a goal. He indicates that
he's going to run this race until the end—he's not
going to let people deceive him. He wants us to
understand that he's pressing and straining because
something wants to hold him back and he wants to
break through. God will get him through.

The reality is many of us are not pressing hard
enough. We have to keep pressing even though the
enemy does not want us to get there, even though we
have doubts and fears. Even when it looks like we
may not make it, people are setting traps and trying
to sabotage us, we still must press on.

In our minds we are in doubt, doubting because
we remember what we used to be, but we have to
press on. It is only when we press on that we will

see what God is actually doing with and through our life. Make sure you understand this. When Paul says to us, "not that I've already obtained all this or already been made perfect," he indicates that you can be saved and not be perfect.

One of the problems within the church is that we look for perfection, and we are critical and judgmental of the moving targets—Jesus, the leadership, and the church. We forget that we won't see perfection until we get to heaven. We are not perfect; if you are looking for perfection in a marriage or job, you will never find it!

Paul says, "I'm pressing on." He says, "I press on to take hold of that." Paul says that he wants to grab it. Grab hold! Maybe Paul had a flashback to Acts, Chapter 9. Then his name was not Paul, but Saul; then he was killing and persecuting the church. All of a sudden, Christ grabbed hold of Saul and turned him around!

Do you remember when Christ grabbed hold of you? You were headed in a direction that was not of God, but God was watching out for you, and He grabbed hold of you before you went too far!

Many people know that I am open about my life. My son got into trouble with the police. He was arrested and put in jail for several misdemeanors, and was supposed to be incarcerated for one year. He prayed for an early release, and when he received it, he called me and said, "Daddy, I really am sorry, and I ask for your forgiveness".

I said, "Son, you are all right; just get back with God."

He replied, "Well, I'm sure glad I prayed! I was blessed with a miracle because they let me go early."

I explained, "No, son, it was not your first blessing. The first blessing was when you got caught! God had to snatch you out of it because if you had kept trying to do what you were doing, you would have been in even more trouble."

My son had lacked commitment to God and his family. Agreement is an important element to commitment.

Remember that you have not always been saved, and you have not always been holy. Remember that there was a night when you thought no one was looking at your mischief, but God was looking, and all of a sudden the Holy Ghost snatched you! Your mother didn't catch you, your father didn't catch you, but God saved you. You need to tell your children the truth about when you were hanging out on the edge of trouble and the Holy Ghost grabbed hold of you in time.

Many of us don't understand where or what our blessing really is. Paul says we must recognize and take hold of it. He says he is not morally perfect; he is a Christian trying to maintain his lifestyle with Christ, to turn into Christ's likeness, and still make it to heaven.

Commitment challenges us all. As I prayed and fasted about this, I asked God to make me more profound, more able to explain how we can avoid the commitment traps so many of us Christians fall into. God laid it in my heart, and He revealed four commitment conditions for the believer that relate to the power of agreement.

First, we face the worldly commitment.

All that you may have learned about worldliness in church classes is true, but I would like for you to go further and step into the natural understanding of worldliness. God's revelation enabled me to break it down differently. Perhaps we are using too many technically religious statements that confuse the issue. There are two definitions of worldliness.

> *You and I have need of the strongest spell that can be found to wake us from the evil enchantment of worldliness.*
> —C.S. Lewis,
> *The Weight of Glory*

It's hard to let go of pleasure!

Many of us have been wrapped in pleasure.

Pleasure isn't limited to sex, drinking, and smoking; those are obvious targets. Instead, let's explore the mind-set of selfish thinking and private selfish pleasures. Perhaps your pleasure is shopping at the mall all day, spending your time and money. Maybe you spend all your extra time (and some that should be spent doing work) watching television or playing video games. That's pleasure, for you.

Yes, we all have given up some things that give us pleasure. But we have hidden our secret pleasures and refuse to give *them* up.

You wonder, "Do you mean I have to give up coffee, smoking, TV, and the chat room?" Yes, if that's where your pleasures are. These private pleasures cause us to wrestle with God regularly. Our indulgences are direct attacks on our agreement with God to be committed to him. The scriptures instruct us to follow this command:

> *Love the Lord your God with all your*
> *heart and with all your soul and with all*
> *your mind and with all your strength.*
> Mark 12:30 (New International Version)

I understand it is hard to give up pleasure, but we must understand that pleasure is worldly.

For some reason we don't believe that there is

pleasure in Jesus! For some reason we don't believe that there is pleasure, fun, and excitement in the church. For some reason we believe that pleasure is only in worldly things.

Whatever God gives you while you're in His house, he will let you keep it with you in your house.

These beliefs could not be farther from the truth. We can have tremendous pleasure in knowing the Lord, in our church, and in many spiritual areas of our lives. We can have fun in Jesus!

It is hard to give up the past. The worldly commitment is not only about pleasure—have you let go of your past? The worldly mind set keeps us in bondage with our past. There is always someone left around to remind us about our past! Our old agreements remind us of what we were, and this gets in the way when we struggle with committing to move forward with God. We must forget what we left behind and press forward.

There will always be someone who sees us standing in church praying. They don't say, "I thank you, Jesus, for what you are doing in my brother or sister's life." They say, "I remember when…." *Forget* "I remember when!"

Now we're in Jesus, and old things have passed away!

Therefore if any person is [ingrafted] in Christ (the Messiah) he is a new creation (a new creature altogether); the old [previous moral and spiritual condition] has passed away. Behold, the fresh and new has come!

2 Corinthians 5:17 (Amplified Bible)

No matter what you think, no matter what you say, don't keep holding on to the good old days. Those days are dead. They weren't as good as you remembered, and they are definitely old!

Don't let your mistakes keep you trapped in your past. Sometimes it's not other people who keep us in bondage, we do it to ourselves. It's hard to understand *"I am a new creation."* I am a new creation, and *I* am still trying to break my old bad habit of using profanity. I know that if I stay with God long enough, eventually my language will become clean.

It's hard for the believer to come to church if you are in the marketplace and have a hustle going. Everything is about a hustle and flow. It's always about a hustle or a hook-up: "Give me a five-finger discount."

You may come to church, but if you don't leave that attitude of hustle behind, the commitment and agreement you still have with your old world won't let you fully absorb the Word. You come to church with your old attitude, and you will not become One with Jesus. Well, let me be honest— I know just how hard it is to leave behind.

A few years ago, my wife and I bought some new furniture from one of my members. My old mindset stepped in. It takes only a minute! I know the challenge of commitment is coming into agreement with God alone, and it produces drive, focus, love, and joy. But when the truck delivered the furniture, I felt like asking the guy if there was anything "thrown off the truck" and available for extra discount. I decided to wait until my furniture was unloaded, and then I would ask.

The driver unloaded the first piece of furniture, and then a second man got off the truck and looked at me. He said, "Hey, I know you. You are Pastor Ogletree!"

Mortified, I groaned, "Oh God!" For a moment I had been in my worldly past again, but God grabbed me in time and said, "Stay with who you are! If you abide in me, and I abide in you, you can ask me for what you want! Drop your worldly hook-up and hook up with the Holy Ghost and see what God will do!"

The "easy way" is always worldly.

We face the carnal commitment.

For they that are after the flesh do mind the things of the flesh; but they that are after the Spirit the things of the Spirit.

For to be carnally minded is death; but to be spiritually minded is life and peace.

Because the carnal mind is enmity against God: for it is not subject to the law of God, neither indeed can be.

So then they that are in the flesh cannot please God.

Romans 8:5-9 (King James Version)

Simply, carnal means unspiritual, under control of ordinary impulses. For some reason, many in the church say that only new members are carnal. That's not so. There are many veterans in the body of the church who sit in the pulpit, or they sit on the front row, or they sing in the choir, but they are still carnal. What do the scriptures mean by that?

If you're carnal, your mind is always stuck in a material, selfish, uncaring, or hypocritical mode.

You can be in church all your life, know the scriptures by heart, and work in the ministry, but if you do not tithe, you are carnal—*you're selfish*. You can be an usher and have the gift of serving, but if you don't hug or smile and truly make others welcome, you are carnal—*you have no gift of fellowship*! As a member at church on Sunday, you shout and hug people, but if you don't check on them during the week, you're carnal—*you're a hypocrite*!

Here's another definition:

> *"Speaking broadly, the carnal denotes the sinful element in man's nature, by reason of descent from Adam; the spiritual is that which comes by the regenerating operation of the Holy Spirit."*
>
> Vine's Expository Dictionary of
> New Testament Words.

The carnal mindset is destroying the church!

What we think we see is not always what we really see.

> *It is written: "I believed; therefore I have spoken." Since we have that same spirit of faith, we also believe and therefore speak, because we know that the one who raised the Lord Jesus from the dead will also raise us with Jesus*

and present us with you to himself. All this is for your benefit, so that the grace that is reaching more and more people may cause thanksgiving to overflow to the glory of God.

Therefore we do not lose heart. Though outwardly we are wasting away, yet inwardly we are being renewed day by day. For our light and momentary troubles are achieving for us an eternal glory that far outweighs them all. So we fix our eyes not on what is seen, but on what is unseen, since what is seen is temporary, but what is unseen is eternal.

2 Corinthians 4:3-18 (New International Version)

Too often, we step into things, not seeing them clearly because we're not looking from God's perspective. Our carnal mind wants to "see" everything first, and this challenges our agreement with God.

Agreement is not always based on sight. We can agree with God without having to see or understand everything.

In order to change our mindset and thought process, we have to change what we see. We need to stop watching what our carnal mind sees, which is only temporary. Let the Holy Spirit fill you and dwell in you. Only then will that which is not seen become seen! Then we will be able to see God's truth for our lives.

Once you're filled with the Holy Spirit, your eyes are open—focused and fixed on the true prize. But the enemy wants to distract you with temporary troubles, tribulations, and difficulties to keep you from prayer, or from fulfilling your commitments to the kingdom. You can be blinded by your own miseries.

Let's look at how a blind spot really works. Cover your left eye with your left hand so you can evaluate your right eye. Hold a pen at arm's length in front of your right eye, and move the pen all the way to your right. You can still see it. Now move the pen all the way to the left. It's now in your blind spot, and you have to trust that it's still there in front of you—you can't see it.

Our spiritual vision is threatened when we look to God and we are distracted because our blind spot—our temporary troubles—are in the way. We take our eyes off the prize. We begin to say, "I don't need to look because it has not happened yet; God has not delivered," and we begin to look elsewhere. We can easily see the opposite side, so we look there instead.

Agreement is not always based on sight. We can agree with God without having to see or understand everything.

God doesn't need to explain his actions and movements. God does strategic and strange things sometimes, and He does not always tell us why He does them. He just says "move," and you need to *move* when He says move. He moves you, and people are watching you. He moves you, and you don't know why.

He sometimes makes you sit in places with people you don't even know. Carnal people may start talking about what happened, and ask questions, "Why did she have to move? What's happening over there? Who told her to come? Why is she here?"

God can move you in church, but He may also tell you to move to another house, another job, another country! It is not for you to question God, and when God says move, you need to stop wondering *why* and just move! Follow Christ, and Christ will take you where you are supposed to go!

God doesn't explain His motives. It's not easy to understand God's motives for moving you. He has them, though! What you do not realize is that you are in danger, wherever you are. The person who lives next door to you is trying to steal your mate, and you don't have a clue. The person on the job whom you trusted with confidential information has been taking the information back to personnel.

It is almost always uncomfortable when God moves you. You are used to being where you are—change is difficult. You are comfortable with the people you already know and the friends you want to see. You are surrounded by the things you are used to seeing. All of a sudden, God takes you out of your safe place and puts you where He wants you.

God only moves you to take you up! He doesn't move you to keep you down; it's always to promote you. God has to move you! God moves you to promote His kingdom through you. He's been moving us since the beginning of time.

> *The Lord had said to Abram, "Go from your country, your people and your father's household to the land I will show you.*
>
> *"I will make you into a great nation, and I will bless you; I will make your name great, and you will be a blessing;*
>
> *I will bless those who bless you, and whoever curses you I will curse; and all*

peoples on earth will be blessed through you."

So Abram went, as the Lord had told him; and Lot went with him. Abram was seventy-five years old when he set out from Harran. He took his wife Sarai, his nephew Lot, all the possessions they had accumulated and the people they had acquired in Harran, and they arrived there.

Genesis 12:1-5 (New International Version)

Sometimes God tells you that you have to separate from those you care about. When God moves you, He does not always plan for everyone to go with you. His road is not always the easy road.

Do you understand why you have to go through so much hell at some point in your life? It is so God can get you to start moving. Some of you are just too afraid to move. The reason you had bad test results from the lab is because God wants you to start moving your lips and begin to praise and thank Him! The reason why you are about to lose your house is because God wants to give you a bigger one! Someone in the church does not understand why he or she is attacking you. It is because

God wants to raise you up over the one who is attacking you!

You don't need to understand His motives. It's enough to know that when God moves you, His motive is to bless you. Agreement must be maintained with God in the unknown times, the unclear times, the hard times, and even the impossible ones.

In 1952, a long-distance swimmer named Florence Chadwick joined a group that planned a swim across the notorious channel between Catalina Island and the California coast. The channel was 21 miles of sharks, icy water, thick fog and strong currents. Florence started her swim strongly, but about an hour and a half in to the race, her hands began to freeze. Her arms were very heavy, and fatigue started to set in. Florence could not see the boats around her when someone shouted "shark attack, shark attack!" and sharks swarmed toward her. The lookouts in the boats shot at the sharks with their rifles and hooked them with their spear guns, and managed to keep the sharks away from her.

Florence's mother and trainer cheered her on by saying, "Just keep on swimming, you are almost there!" She kept going, dug down into her reserves, and swam. By the time she swam 20 miles, her hands were completely frozen, and she could barely move her arms. The cold water was slapping her in the face, and the waves were high. She was one mile from shore, and her mother and trainer shouted again, "Keep on swimming; you are almost there!"

Florence was so cold! She couldn't see the boats or the shore. Suddenly she simply gave up and stopped swimming—she gave up. Florence was only one mile from the shore when they pulled her into the boat and began to warm her up. They rubbed her down with warm towels and tried to raise her body temperature as they brought her to shore. As she began to catch her breath, a reporter ran up to her and asked, "Florence, what happened! You were so close!" Florence replied, "I quit because I could not see the shore."

Imagine you are swimming toward the shore, and are ready to give up. Imagine God tells you, *"I am going to bless you, you must keep on swimming!"* Imagine He says, *"I am going to elevate you, you must keep fighting!"* Imagine He says, *"Victory is yours! Keep on moving until you see the shore!"*

Men may not always keep their agreements with you, but God does. With Him, it is a done deal.

There is danger in a half-hearted commitment.

*Blessed (happy, fortunate, to be envied)
are those who dwell in Your house* and
*Your presence; they will be singing Your
praises all the day long. Selah [pause,
and calmly think of that]!*

Psalm 84:4 (Amplified Bible)

Many of us don't understand that *blessed* means
happy; *blessed* means prosperous. You are blessed
as long as you're in God's house. You may not feel
blessed in your own house, but that's one of the
reasons you need to keep coming to God's house!
Whatever God gives you while you're in His house,
he will let you keep it with you in your house.

Sometimes we come to church, but we are not
happy in Jesus. We are not happy because our house
or job, our children or whatever goes on outside in
the world weighs us down. When that happens, we
become committed in only a half-hearted way. When
we're half-hearted in our commitment, we have one
foot in the house with Jesus and one foot out. We have
one foot with Jesus and one foot with Satan. We take
one step with Jesus and two steps with our friends.

Paul says to us that we can't have a half-hearted
commitment:

But let him ask in faith, nothing wavering. For he that wavereth is like a wave of the sea driven with the wind and tossed.

For let not that man think that he shall receive any thing of the Lord.

A double minded man is unstable in all his ways.

James 1:6-8 (King James Version)

God told me people are proud of being church members, but these same people demand that their church not expect anything from them except their attendance. This is the case in most churches, including mine.

A Purpose-Driven Life is an excellent book by Rick Warren. He has broken his book into 40 short chapters, one to be read and studied each day. Day 17 describes the difference between a church attendee and a committed member. Attendees want all the benefits of the church. They want the right hand of fellowship, they want benevolence, and they want a hug from the pastor. If they don't get it, they grumble, "He's not wholly supporting me today."

Do you recognize yourself as someone who

wants to be known as part of the group that eats out with the pastor and the leaders, but if you're not invited, you say they're stuck up and you stay away? You will go visit some other church; as a matter of fact, you are just going to watch TV because it is football season.

On the other hand, a true member understands that their responsibility is to protect the church, to *be a part of the church.* The fully committed member has responsibilities and will not malign their church or pastor. How can a committed member curse the house he or she is trying to be blessed in? He who dwells in the house of the Lord shall be blessed!

Too many of us are half-hearted with our commitment, and we want to attend when *we* want to attend, just maybe communion Sundays. When we attend on the weeks we don't get paid, we use that as an excuse for not paying our tithes. Half-hearted members believe that since they signed their name as "member" they are really members. No, that person is an attendee! Agreement is deeper than membership.

Agreement must be maintained with God in the unknown times, the unclear times, the hard times, and even the impossible ones.

An attendee says, "I do what I want to do," but that is not how the church is designed. Attendees say, "I'll attend when I want to attend." Will they attend heaven the way they want to? Will they even get there?

Attendees don't want to be assigned to a ministry unless it's one they like, not considering its functional or dysfunctional role. Since attendees feel like they're on the outside, they're more likely to talk negatively. Attendees don't want to be assigned to class because they think they already know it all.

The members of the church are the body of Christ. Our confession in Jesus is to move into agreement, with Christ being the Lord of our lives. The commitment we make to him moves us into an assignment to accomplish God's purpose for kingdom growth.

God is always moving, so there are always changes in what we use in the church and information we share. The church started evolving after Jesus departed, and it's been changing ever since. There are new dreams, new thoughts and new concepts in the church. Members share these dreams and grow in the church.

Attendees also believe that they can't give their "resources." How little these ignorant people know! The reality is, if you *really* come to Christ, you know that your "resources" are not yours, *they belong to God.* You are just a manager, a steward over what God has loaned you. Your house is not really your house; your name is on it, but the seal of the Holy Ghost is covering you, and that is not yours!

Realize these are not *your* children; this is not *your* husband. You need to say, "I gave all of this to you, God," and mean it with a whole heart, not half of your heart.

Agreement is deeper than membership. Attendees may say, "I'm going to offer my time when I want to." You really don't have time to wait for a convenient time! **When He comes back, will you be ready?**

The danger within the church is we have too many people who are half-hearted, who love the church today, but hate the church the next day. They are walking a dangerous line.

The commitment of faithfulness.

We will end on a great and encouraging note: God knows all of our weaknesses and He's moving us from being worldly, carnal and half-hearted. He is moving us into faithfulness.

Why should we be faithful? Grace and mercy! You know about grace and mercy. Let's read the psalm that everyone knows and loves the most:

> The LORD *is my shepherd; I shall not want.*

He maketh me to lie down in green pastures: he leadeth me beside the still waters.

He restoreth my soul: he leadeth me in the paths of righteousness for his name's sake.

Yea, though I walk through the valley of the shadow of death, I will fear no evil: for thou art with me; thy rod and thy staff they comfort me.

Thou preparest a table before me in the presence of mine enemies: thou anointest my head with oil; my cup runneth over.

Surely goodness and mercy shall follow me all the days of my life: and I will dwell in the house of the LORD *for ever.*

Psalm 23 (King James Version)

I especially love this part of the last verse: *Goodness and mercy shall follow me all the days of my life.* I asked God why goodness and mercy didn't lead the way instead of follow. He said, "Because of all of the mistakes you've made, they have to go behind you to cover up and hide all the times you have done wrong. They have to hide anger, bitterness. They have to cover up all of your messes, because in reality, if goodness and mercy were in the front, we would not follow them."

Why do I remain faithful? Goodness and mercy. I was worldly, but today I'm in Christ Jesus. Once I was carnal, but now I've changed. When we understand faithfulness, we will run this race.

People feel the need to feel a part of something big and famous, like being fans of a football or basketball team. They identify with the team and wear their colors, and they cheer when the team is winning. If they boo and empty out the stadium when their team is losing, though, they're only fair-weather, half-hearted fans. They're not faithful.

Half-hearted, faithless attendees do the same at church: They cheer when you are winning and boo you when you are losing.

> *Do you not know that in a race all the runners run, but only one gets the prize? Run in such a way as to get the prize. Everyone who competes in the games goes into strict training. They do it to get a crown that will not last, but we do it to get a crown that will last forever.*

1 Corinthians 9:24-25 (New International Version)

Get it in your spirit and say to yourself, "If I am going to run this race, I will run this race correctly." Run this race to the finish; get the prize that He has for you. You need to understand the prize is not a crown for this world. The prize is not a job; the prize is not to be seen on stage. The prize is the crown you will receive in heaven.

God tells you to run your race using the original Greek philosophy of the Olympics. When you ran in the first Greek marathons, it did not matter if you came in first; it mattered only if your torch was still lit when you finished!

Many of us are in the race but our torch is not lit. We have no fire, we have no energy, and we don't feel like committing! Many of us have not been faithful, and we make so many different excuses. God understands that people work; He understands that some of you have children and many demands on your time and wallets. He understands you are unbearably stressed, but you have to remain faithful. You still have to run this race.

> It is always too soon to quit!
> —Norman Vincent Peale

It is amazing how one Sunday we are supportive and cheer when we hear about praise and prosperity. The next week, when the pastor talks about commitment, there is no cheering going on—just silence.

Derek Redmond was selected to represent Great Britain in the 1988 Seoul Olympics. He had trained for the 400-meter race for years and held many medals records, but 90 seconds before his first Olympic heat, he tore a ligament and had to withdraw.

Over the next four years, he had many surgeries. In 1992, Derek qualified for the Barcelona Olympics, and his father came along to watch and support him. In his first heat, Derek came in first place and was leading the scoreboard. In the quarterfinals, he won his heat. Before he started the semifinals, Derek looked up to the stands and saw his father; he knew he had a chance to win it. He remembered what he had trained for. He remembered how he had faced injuries but he knew and believed that this was his year.

The gun went off. Derek took off and he was running as fast as he could but about 250 meters from the finish, his hamstring snapped and he fell to the ground. Writhing in pain, Derek saw the other runners cross the finish line. He refused a stretcher, saying, "No, I am going to finish this race," and he got up and started to limp painfully to the finish line. 65,000 people in the stadium crowd stood up and cheered him on, and millions of others cheered in their own living rooms.

A man ran through the crowd, burst past security and ran down the track to Derek. Someone told the announcer it was Derek's father, and the crowd cheered them both as the father supported his son as he limped down the stadium track. When they got to the finish line, his father stepped back and let Derek cross over by himself. The crowd yelled that Derek won! They were amazed and appreciative that he did not give up.

Don't give up before the miracle happens.
—Fannie Flagg

Jesus Christ ran a race for 33 years, and people loved Him and people cursed Him. Let's remember Jesus as He ran his last lap, the week before they crucified Him. One crowd cheered Him, saying "Hosanna!" Another crowd booed Him, screaming "Crucify Him!"

Jesus had a Judas in His camp and a Peter in His camp; those who had trained with Him had forsaken Him. We know for sure our Lord and Savior died on that night. He was out of the race and it looked as though He was not going to make it. He Himself even said, "It is finished."

Then the Father in heaven came down, and He put His arms around Jesus in the tomb. In an instant,

God let Jesus cross over from time into eternity, from death into light. You should shout and cheer because Jesus made it! His resurrection is our guarantee that we can make it too.

Conclusion

$\mathcal{L}$et's briefly review our travels down the path of becoming a leader in the kingdom. It is not a solitary path, and we travel in agreement with many others, especially with God.

Jesus speaks about the power and importance of agreement, which we've discussed from several viewpoints in these chapters.

> *Again, I tell you that if two of you on earth agree about anything you ask for, it will be done for you by my Father in heaven. For where two or three come together in my name, there am I with them.*
>
> Matthew 18:19-20 (New International Version)

First we studied how God desired and designed the covenant of agreement, and we followed several Old Testament figures as they learned what He meant and expected. We saw the repercussions experienced by the Israelites when they broke their agreement with Him, and when Joseph shared his dream with his brothers too soon.

God has plans for us too, and we must agree to follow the dream He gives us so we have a purpose in life.

We know we must support others' dreams and not tear them down. When we support and agree with our spouses and are prepared to go the distance, we'll have harmony within the home and that will help us manage our dreams. Two are better than one, especially handling the responsibilities we share raising a family.

We learned more about strongholds: We know our churches need our protection and we need to man the walls ourselves, evangelize and *never* sell out. Strongholds can also be prisons rather than protection, when we lock ourselves in to avoid change and challenge. Fear and ignorance keep many people locked in a prison, away from God. Inside the church, the movement of the Holy Spirit will help break the stronghold of people's negativity and misery.

Change is good! Change happens when we're provoked and agitated. The church is not meant just to comfort us and protect us from the enemy. The Spirit of God will fill us and exalt us as we embrace and rise to the challenge to change. The church has always been about change; the bible teaches this through the ministry of Jesus Christ.

Then we discussed unity and the power of One. Our words and our spirit should match; our relationships should be about spiritual connections, not only for material enhancements. Diversity—embracing the many different individuals that become one stronger entity—is important to the health of our unity and the church.

Falsity is infectious—but so is the Holy Spirit! We need to make sure we aren't just concerned with the appearance of being saved. There is no unity when the Spirit of God doesn't live within us. Study the Word of God so we have the wisdom and the power to overcome our challenges.

We need to bless others and not attack them, and expand our circle of prayer to pray for the church, the community, and the country. The kingdom always needs to come first. Our prayers should always be for God's presence; when He is with us, our success is guaranteed. Agreement and Oneness will bring the Spirit of God to cleanse and baptize us in the fire.

Two chapters were dedicated to commitment. Reciprocity by others is not guaranteed, but that is not a valid excuse to shirk our part of the agreement, whether it's a job or a relationship. Personal relationships are becoming more fragile as people just walk away with no sense of commitment. People use the same lame excuses to avoid going to church or having a ministry, or committing their works to the Lord.

The discovery process—being honest with ourselves—helps us perfect our commitment. Even though we're torn with demands from those we love and from those for whom we work, our minds must remain focused on the object of our commitment. Our focus had better be on the Lord, no matter how distracted and burdened we are with other problems.

> *Commit your work to the Lord,*
> *then it will succeed.*
>
> Proverbs 16:3 (The Living Bible).

Once we make that commitment, we must press on—we can't quit, or doubt, or worry. When we press on, we will see what God plans for our life. Even if we're saved, there is work to be done, for we're not perfect until we get to heaven. There is no perfection unless it is in heaven—certainly not in our spouse or in our earthly lives.

At some point in our lives, God reached out and grabbed us before we went too far in our old ways. We need to thank God that he was committed to our future, even though we were not committed to him.

We need to let go of our selfish pleasures, and let go of the past. The good old days were dangerous ones for us. We are a new creation, and we no longer need our old bad habits. We are to be spiritual now, rather than carnal. As we work to be unselfish, full of fellowship and love, and true to our agreement with God, we must make sure the good old days don't pull us back.

Once the Holy Spirit fills us and dwells in us, we will see God's truth for our lives. We will not be blinded by our temporary troubles.

God's plans often involve change and movement, which almost always is uncomfortable. His road is never the easy road, but it will lead you to better things. His motive is always to bless you and to reward you—never to punish you. You just can't lose sight of our commitment to God, to the church, our families and to ourselves to effect the change needed to come into agreement with God.

The commitment of being a member of the church—not just an attendee!—is worthy of a great deal of discussion. Too many "members" are half-hearted in their commitment and are really just attendees: They don't tithe, they don't take the ministries they're given, they talk negatively. They are not faithful; they don't do the work, they don't learn and prepare for change. Attendees will not be ready when the time comes for His return.

Don't be a half-hearted attendee and forget your agreement with God. Others are looking to you as a leader and will follow your example. Do the work! Trust Him and remember He created you in His image so he can walk in agreement with you. Stay *fully* committed to Him. Remember the prize is in heaven, not on this earth.